Equity-Indexed Annuities:

The Smart Consumer's Guide

Equity-Indexed Annuities:

The Smart Consumer's Guide

Jay D. Adkisson, JD

iUniverse, Inc.
New York Lincoln Shanghai

Equity-Indexed Annuities: *The Smart Consumer's Guide*

Copyright © 2006 by Jay D. Adkisson

All rights reserved. No part of this book may be used or reproduced by any means, graphic, electronic, or mechanical, including photocopying, recording, taping or by any information storage retrieval system without the written permission of the publisher except in the case of brief quotations embodied in critical articles and reviews.

iUniverse books may be ordered through booksellers or by contacting:

iUniverse
2021 Pine Lake Road, Suite 100
Lincoln, NE 68512
www.iuniverse.com
1-800-Authors (1-800-288-4677)

ISBN-13: 978-0-595-40418-6 (pbk)
ISBN-13: 978-0-595-84794-5 (ebk)
ISBN-10: 0-595-40418-9 (pbk)
ISBN-10: 0-595-84794-3 (ebk)

Printed in the United States of America

Contents

ABOUT THE AUTHOR vii
PREFACE. xi
CHAPTER 1   INTRODUCTION 1
CHAPTER 2   INTEREST CREDITING: THE MINIMUM RETURN 8
CHAPTER 3   INDEX CREDITING: THE MAXIMUM RETURN 12
CHAPTER 4   INDEXING METHODS. 18
CHAPTER 5   PAYOUT METHODS. 24
CHAPTER 6   THE ANNUITY COMPANY 27
CHAPTER 7   SUITABILITY ISSUES: COMPLEXITY, DISCLOSURE, LIQUIDITY AND WITHDRAWALS 30
CHAPTER 8   PORTFOLIO ROLE OF EIAS 36
CHAPTER 9   TAX CONSIDERATIONS 41
CHAPTER 10   ASSET PROTECTION 46
CHAPTER 11   QUESTIONS AND MORE INFORMATION. 49
APPENDIX A   National Association of Securities Dealers (NASD) Equity-Indexed Annuities—A Complex Choice . 53

APPENDIX B   National Association of Insurance Commissioners
             (NAIC) Buyer's Guide To Equity-Indexed
             Annuities 59
APPENDIX C   U.S. Securities & Exchange Commission (SEC)
             Equity-Indexed Annuities. 71
Index 75

ABOUT THE AUTHOR

Jay D. Adkisson is currently the Director of Private Client Services of Select Portfolio Management, Inc., a registered investment advisory with offices in Aliso Viejo, California. Mr. Adkisson is also a Registered Options Principal for Securities Equity Group, Inc., a securities broker-dealer, with NASD Series 4, 7, 63 and 65. Mr. Adkisson is licensed as a Life Agent with the California Department of Insurance, No. 0D50858.

An attorney since 1989, Mr. Adkisson is a Partner of Riser Adkisson LLP with main offices in Atlanta, Georgia. He has been admitted to practice in Oklahoma, Texas, and various federal courts nationwide. He is a member in good standing of the Oklahoma Bar Association, the State Bar of Texas, and the American Bar Association.

Mr. Adkisson is the co-author, with his law partner Mr. Chris Riser, of "Asset Protection: Concepts and Strategies" which is currently published by McGraw-Hill & Co. He was also a contributor to the second volume of the American Bar Association compendium on asset protection and the author of numerous professional articles and reports on asset protection, trusts, business entities, and creditor-debtor law.

Mr. Adkisson has twice appeared as an expert witness to the U.S. Senate Finance Committee, been the feature of an article in *Forbes* magazine, and is routinely quoted in the Wall Street Journal, the Financial Times, and New York Times, and various other newspapers and media outlets nationwide on financial and tax scams and asset protection issues. Mr. Adkisson is perhaps best known internationally as the creator of Quatloos.com which is popular for educating the general public about various financial scams and tax frauds. He has regularly volunteered his time to lecture to various civic groups and to educate agents of the Internal Revenue Service about abusive tax schemes.

Mr. Adkisson has Bachelor of Arts and Juris Doctor degrees from the University of Oklahoma, and was a member of the Oklahoma Law Review.

After losing an eye to cancer in 2000, Mr. Adkisson created LostEye.com to provide support to those who had also lost sight in one eye. He has recently authored a book "Lost Eye: Coping with Monocular Vision after Enucleation or Eye Loss from Cancer, Accident, or Disease" which describes the experience of losing an eye as related by Mr. Adkisson and others in hopes of helping other people through this difficult time.

Mr. Adkisson is a much sought-after speaker on wealth planning topics and has made presentations to the American Bar Association, various state and local bar associations nationwide, and other professional organizations.

Mr. Adkisson is available as a speaker on the proper use of equity-indexed annuities, the use of equity-indexed annuities in advanced estate and asset protection planning, and similar topics.

The statements, views, positions and observations herein are those of Jay D. Adkisson only, and do not represent the statements, views, positions, or observations of any other persons or entities, including Select Portfolio Management, Inc., Securities Equity Group, Inc., Riser Adkisson LLP, Adkisson Publishing, Inc., or Financial & Tax Fraud Education Associates, Inc.

ACKNOWLEDGMENTS

Thanks go to Tony Amaradio, Dan Amaradio, Semir Amin, and Mark Goldsmith for their helpful comments and suggestions. Thanks also to Joe Petrucelli and Chris Riser for their assistance on the chapter relating to tax issues. Thanks to insurance consultant JJ McNabb for forwarding to me very helpful information about the regulation of equity-indexed annuities. As with my two previous books, thanks goes to my father Ron Adkisson for his work as my editor and advisor.

PREFACE

Both as the Director of Private Client Services for my investment advisory firm, Select Portfolio Management, and as the Editor of my popular website that debunks financial frauds and tax scams, Quatloos.com, I am frequently asked this question: "What should I put my money in if I want better than CD rates, but I don't want the chance of losing any money?"

In the past, there weren't many good answers to this question other than to buy high-grade bonds and plan on holding them to maturity. There are two problems with this. The first is that bonds spin off taxes every year. The second is that the price of bonds can go down as well as up, meaning that the bonds might have to be held to maturity to realize their desired yield.

In 1995, near the height of the mutual fund boom, Keyport Life introduced the first equity-indexed annuity. This was about the time the dot.com bull market started to run, and then turned into a full-fledged bubble as investors convinced themselves of the "new economic paradigm" of the internet economy. This new market could never go down! By contrast, the relatively conservative returns paid by equity-indexed annuities seemed unattractive and they failed to develop market traction.

Eventually, the bubble burst—assisted in substantial part by the 9/11 terrorist act and revelations of the scandals at Enron, WorldCom, Tyco, and other major corporations. This left many retirees wondering why their Golden Nest Eggs had broken. They realized for the first time that the internal diversification of mutual funds didn't provide much protection as almost everything went down in a hurry. The mutual fund honeymoon was over. Consumers needed a solution, and one without market risk.

It was only in the brutal bear markets of 2001 and 2002 did equity-indexed annuities really start to take off and, by the time of the writing of this book, they had spawned an industry where annual sales were measured in the tens-of-billions of dollars. Equity-indexed annuities are currently marketed to those who are understandably risk-adverse.

While the number of equity-indexed annuity products has dramatically increased, there has been little more done in the way of educating the average consumer about what these products are and how they work. Certainly, the

NAIC, NASD and SEC have issued some excellent short publications, but these give only the broadest overview of equity-indexed annuities without providing real guidance on the issues that consumers should be the most concerned about.

My purpose in writing this book was to fill the education gap and to provide the information the average consumer needs to know before placing money into equity-indexed annuities. Hopefully, the agents and advisors who sell or recommend equity-indexed annuities will give their clients a copy of this book prior to their signing the contract and handing over a check, so that any confusion or misconceptions are spotted in advance and there are no misunderstandings discovered later.

Equity-indexed annuities can be wonderful and safe products when used correctly, but the responsibility for assuring that they are used correctly is shared by both the selling agent and the consumer. Nobody knows the consumer's particular circumstances and needs better than the consumer. This book advises consumers of their responsibilities to know when an equity-indexed annuity is right for them, and to also know what contractual terms and conditions, as well as basic tax treatment, they must be aware of prior to purchasing a particular annuity.

This book is not meant to be a definitive treatment of all of the regulatory, tax, and financial issues involving either equity-indexed annuities in particular or annuities in general. Nor does this book seek to catalogue all types of EIAs or even the many methods for linking products to the index. Any attempt to describe or catalogue each of these methods in any depth would increase the size of this book tenfold, and defeat its purpose as a general guide. Rather, the goal of this book is to get the average consumer to the place where he or she can intelligently understand a single contract and its associated marketing brochure, and ask the selling agent meaningful questions, but not to compare all the numerous available products and their variations.

To an extent, this book is also written for my numerous journalist friends who regularly call looking for information that would help them to understand these products. I usually point out that equity-indexed annuities are much easier to understand if they are seen simply as an advanced form of a fixed annuity (which they are), as opposed to a confusing version of a variable annuity (which they are not).

Indeed, at times it seems like even some regulators do not understand equity-indexed annuities and superficially attempt to treat them as a form of variable annuity, even though they are nothing like a variable annuity. Perhaps this book will help them to better understand equity-indexed annuities as well.

I very much look forward to readers' feedback on the issues that are discussed herein and any suggestions as to how this book may be improved in future editions.

Jay D. Adkisson
Orange County, California, 2006

1
INTRODUCTION

The *Equity-Indexed Annuity* (EIA) is one of the best retirement tools developed in recent years. An EIA guarantees that you will at least get your initial premiums back if you hold it past the surrender period. But by a linking feature to a major stock index, the EIA has the realistic chance of growing faster than traditional forms of annuities.

In circumstances where an EIA is suitable, it can be a product that protects you from the loss of your premium if the markets crash, yet also allows you to gain better returns if the stock markets perform well. Because of this safety, EIAs can be a good purchase for those approaching retirement and who cannot afford to lose their savings, yet still would like the chance for better returns than those paid by Certificates of Deposits or money market funds.

Even for those who will not strictly need the money for their retirement, EIAs are an attractive long-term product for those who want to approach the markets conservatively and do not want any market risk. EIAs can also play a role in intelligently designing diversified portfolios.

As we shall see, there is almost no significant downside to buying an EIA so long as certain suitability criteria are met. But there is no free lunch on Wall Street, and EIAs do have substantial holding periods and surrender charges as discussed in detail below. These should not keep you from buying an EIA so long as you realize that your purchase of EIAs will be a long term affair, and you do not anticipate needing cash from your EIA during the surrender period.

The purpose of this book is not to advocate EIAs as the perfect annuity product. Rather, it is to examine a financial tool that should be considered by more consumers because of EIAs' inherent safety. This is especially true as many Americans are finding out that their retirement savings may be inadequate for their future needs, and will thus need better rates of growth to close their personal pension gap.

Too many consumers who can ill afford losses are taking unnecessary risks by being in the stock markets and risking the loss of their principal. Many retirees who lost their savings in the dot.com crash can sympathize with this result, and now understand the folly of their investment advisors encouraging them into over-aggressive market participation when they should have been putting their eggs into safer nests.

On the other hand, EIAs have sometimes been sold in situations where they were unsuitable. The usual circumstance is the consumer who, at the time they purchased the EIA, knew or should have known that they would need cash from the EIA during the surrender period. The agent knew that the consumer needed their money within this period, but sold them the EIA anyway.

Finally, a significant problem with EIAs is their inherent complexity. All EIAs have one or more "moving parts" (terms that can change) and it is sometimes difficult for even experienced sales agents to fully understand how certain products work. Unless you are an expert on EIAs, you have little chance of truly comprehending all of the ramifications of what you are buying and this can later lead to confusion and unfortunate results. Thus, another significant purpose of this book is to identify the issues that you most need to know about so that you can ask the right questions of your agent or advisor.

For many consumers, however, and especially those who are understandably gun-shy of the possibility of losing money in the stock market, EIAs offer substantial upside potential without downside market risk. So what is an EIA and how does it work?

What is an Annuity?

An *annuity* is an income stream consisting of regular payments that are made to you either for some agreed period (such as 20 years) or until your death. If you are the one who has the right to the income stream, you are known as the *owner*. If the annuity is measured on your life, then you are known as the *annuitant*. You can be either the owner or the annuitant, or both the owner and the annuitant in regard to a particular annuity.

Annuities are primarily intended to provide money for retirement, as opposed to life insurance that is meant to provide money for heirs. The most common annuity is one that would make payments to you until you die. The annuity payments would be calculated based on your life expectancy: The annuity company would win if you died early and would lose if you lived past your life expectancy.

Contrast this with life insurance where the life insurance company loses if you die early and would win if you lived past your life expectancy. In this respect, annuities and life insurance are on opposite sides of the same coin, with that coin being the risk that you will die early or live too long.[1]

With better medical care and healthier living, the greatest fear of many Americans is that they will outlive their retirement savings. Between long-term concerns about the Social Security system and underfunded corporate pension arrangements, this fear has some validity.

Fixed Annuity

Fundamentally, an EIA is a *fixed annuity*. You give the annuity company an amount of money, and the annuity company will spread its payments back to you for either a certain period or for the rest of your life.[2] With an EIA, these payments are deferred for a term of years during which the annuity grows. This is more fully explained below.

Most EIAs are also a *declared rate fixed annuity*. This means that instead of the annuity company giving you a single set rate for the life of the annuity, the annuity company will annually publish an interest rate that is being paid. This rate can never be a negative number. The annuity company's method of crediting interest to the EIA is detailed much more fully later in Chapter 4 relating to Indexing Methods.

Like any other fixed annuity, an EIA guarantees you that whatever else happens, so long as you hold the EIA past the surrender period you will not lose your principal and you will have at least your premium payments returned to you. This is the biggest single advantage of an EIA—in part, what you are purchasing with an EIA is peace-of-mind.

Similarly, EIAs typically have no "internal expenses". In other words, they do not have internal charges, fees, or front-end or back-end loads that will drag the performance of an EIA. With an EIA, your return will literally be "What You See Is What You Get". Contrast this with variable annuities, mutual funds, and managed accounts that have various fees and expenses that can significantly drag their investment performance over time.

---

1. As a matter of semantics, annuities are really "life insurance" in the sense that they take care of you if you live too long, while life insurance is really "death insurance" that takes care of your heirs if you do not live long enough.
2. An annuity can be structured so that it pays out for the entirety of your life or the life of your spouse, whoever lives the longest.

Deferral, Accumulation and Distribution

An EIA is also a *deferred annuity*, which means that the annuity does not begin making annuity payments to you immediately,[3] but instead its payments do not begin until some future date from the date of purchase. This deferral allows the annuity to grow until the time when the value of the annuity is needed. This deferral period is referred to as the *accumulation phase* since the value of the annuity will be increasing during this period.

Many EIAs allow limited quarterly or annual "free withdrawals" without forcing the annuity payments to start or without triggering surrender penalties. These withdrawals can assist with cash-flow needs during the accumulation phase. Of course, the taking of "free withdrawals" means that there may be less money in the contract to earn interest and this could lower the amount that is ultimately paid out.

The period when the annuity is no longer growing but instead is making payments to you is known as the *distribution phase*. During this period, the value of the annuity will be decreasing. The owner's decision to start having regular payments made is known as *annuitization*. This is discussed further in Chapter 5 on Payout Methods.

Equity-Indexed Annuities

If the stock markets crashed, or simply went flat, during the accumulation phase of the EIA, the EIA would simply operate like a traditional fixed annuity. You would still get the benefit of the published interest rate, the tax deferral, and annuity payments for a period certain or until you die. But if the stock markets take off, you have the chance to earn much more because of the EIA's "upside only" linkage to the index.

All EIAs track a stock market index, most commonly the Standard & Poor's index of the stock values in 500 of the largest and most representative corporations, known as the *S&P 500*[4]. If the tracked index substantially increases during the term of the EIA, the value of the EIA will also increase to some degree. We say "to some degree" because few EIAs track the index exactly, and there is a wide variety of methods used by the annuity company to correlate the gains of a particular EIA against the tracked index. These methods are considered more fully in Chapter 4 relating to Indexing Methods.

---

3. An annuity that starts to pay out within a year of when the annuity payments are made is known as an *immediate annuity*.
4. The "S&P 500" is a registered trademark of McGraw-Hill & Co.

Note that the index linking feature of EIAs is purely a bonus, since there is no downside if the index performs poorly other than that the interest rate will apply instead of the equity index rate. EIAs are fundamentally fixed annuities, but at the end of the period you will receive the larger of the yield based on an equity index or the interest rate.

Contrast with Variable Annuities

The most common mistake by those who are attempting to evaluate equity-indexed annuities is to compare them to a *variable annuity* (VA), which EIAs are not, instead of to other forms of fixed annuities, which EIAs are. At times, it seems like some critics of EIAs intentionally blur the differences between the products so that EIAs are unfairly tarred with the stigma that attaches to variable annuities.

A variable annuity is an annuity contract that tracks the stock market directly, and its value can go down if the market sinks. The value of a VA contract is determined by a *separate account* that holds a bucket of diverse investments (usually which mirror popular mutual funds) for each individual contract. Variable annuities usually require ongoing portfolio management to make sure that your bucket is in the right investments.

There is a huge difference between equity-indexed annuities and variable annuities: VAs have full market performance (and full market risk), and EIAs do not. There simply is no long-term minimum guarantee with a variable annuity, except that some VA contracts promise to return at least your premium at death or sometimes for a short period of years after purchase. With a variable annuity, you can literally lose all of your initial investment if the markets go down and stay down. Contrast this with an EIA, where at least your initial premium payment will be returned to you when held past the surrender period.

One might loosely analogize EIAs to a "variable annuity that can't go down" but to do so would overlook other important differences between EIAs and variable annuities, such as that VAs internally charge all sorts of fees and expenses, such as management fees. These fees and expenses drag the investment performance of the VA annually. By contrast, EIAs typically have no internal fees or expenses and so your return is "What You See Is What You Get" according to the terms of the contract.

Surrender Charges

All EIAs have penalties if there is an early large withdrawal. These are known as *Surrender Charges*. These charges will start high and then decline over time. For instance, they may be 12% in the first year, 11% in the second year, etc., and decline each year until there are no penalties. The time during which surrender charges apply is known as the *Surrender Period.*

Because EIAs have no internal expenses, the annuity company must pay its own expenses and such things as trading costs and the agent's commissions from its long-term profits based on investing your premiums.[5] The surrender charges help to ensure that the annuity company will make this long-term profit by discouraging withdrawals in the early years. If a large withdrawal is made from the EIA during the surrender period, then the annuity company gets the surrender charges, but if no withdrawals are made during this period then the annuity company gets its long-term profit.[6]

If the EIA is annuitized (*i.e.,* the stream of regular payments from the annuity is started) or if the annuitant dies during the surrender period, then the surrender charges will typically not apply.

Nothing usually happens at the end of the surrender period, except that surrender charges no longer apply. Note that some EIAs with end-point designs may automatically re-start the period (and the surrender charges) at the end of the sur-

---

5. The amount of commissions paid to the agent who sells an EIA has no direct impact upon the stated performance of the EIA. Very simply, the EIA pays what the EIA pays, without consideration of the commission. If the EIA pays a minimum of 3%, then it pays a minimum of 3% without any deduction for the commission. If the EIA pays a maximum of 7%, then it pays a maximum of 7% without any deduction for the commission. *What You See Is What You Get.* It simply doesn't matter if the agent gets a commission of 3%, 8%, 25% or 75% or 500% of the amount of the premium—the EIA itself will still perform as promised. *What You See Is What You Get.* The commissions certainly may affect interest rates, participation rates, caps, the length of surrender periods, and other features, but this impact occurs before the terms are offered to the investor, and not after.

   Many things go into how annuity companies calculate the agent's commissions that have nothing to do with the particular EIA that is sold. Some annuity companies feel that they have to pay large commissions to compete with the management fees that financial planners consider themselves to lose when an EIA investment is made. Over the lifetime of the EIA contract, these lost management fees can be substantial, and is usually a significant hidden motivation for criticisms expressed by some financial planners against EIAs.

   The real issue with commissions is an issue of agent suitability, *i.e.,* whether the agent is allowing the promise of significant commissions to cloud the determination whether EIAs are suitable for a particular investor. As mentioned throughout, a key to successfully investing in EIAs is to find an agent who is very familiar with these products, understands them, and has strict guidelines for suitability.

render period unless you elect to annuitize or exchange the annuity. The end of the surrender period is often erroneously called the "Term" of the annuity, although the real term of the annuity ends on the *Maturity Date*, which will be something like "age 100".

The relationship of surrender charges to when an EIA should or should not be purchased is discussed further in Chapter 7.

---

6. Note that many EIA contracts may allow limited "free withdrawals" without penalty during the surrender charge period, such as 10% of the contract value per year. However, these "free withdrawals" may impact the long-term gains that will be paid since no future interest will be paid on the amounts that are withdrawn.

2

INTEREST CREDITING: THE MINIMUM RETURN

All EIAs pay a certain minimum guaranteed rate, so that regardless of what happens with the index you will know with certainty the minimum amount of money that you will receive at the end of the contract so long as you do not withdraw any funds early. This minimum guaranteed rate is known as the "floor". Of all the provisions of an EIA contract, understanding this minimum guaranteed rate is very important since it is the only return that you can really count on.

A common floor is 0%, meaning that at the end of the contract term you will get back at least the same amount of money that you paid into the contract as premiums. With such a contract you have no risk of losing principal, which allows you to dip your toe into the stock markets by way of the index linkage (but without losing your toe if the markets decline).

Insurance companies may decide to pay a higher than minimum rate during the contract term in order to make their products look more attractive to consumers. However, any higher rate currently being paid by the annuity company over the floor should not be considered for purposes of anticipating the "absolute return" value of the EIA—which value should always be presumed to be the guaranteed minimum.[7]

You may be better off with a lower minimum guaranteed rate, however, since with some contracts this may allow the annuity company to offer better participation in the index-linked return. Since over the long term the index-linked return should normally outperform the minimum guaranteed rate (which in many ways is more like a safety parachute than your hoped-for return), taking a higher

---

7. Note that once the index crediting method has credited an amount greater than the minimum guaranteed return, then the minimum guaranteed return becomes totally irrelevant as you will always receive the *higher* return.

indexed payout against a lower minimum guaranteed rate might be a good bet in some circumstances.

Another issue that you must understand is when the minimum guaranteed rate will be credited. Some contracts will only credit the interest payment at the end of the surrender period. Thus, withdrawals against the policy in the interim may not receive even the minimum interest return, and the long-term return of that EIA will be correspondingly lowered. Caution that withdrawals made prior to the end of the contract may adversely affect this floor and create the potential for loss of principal, see *Suitability Issues,* in Chapter 7. We cannot repeat enough that an EIA is not a suitable purchase for you if you will need to make large withdrawals from them prior to the end of the contract term.[8]

Participation Rates

Crediting is a difficult concept that can significantly affect the ultimate returns paid by the EIA. Do not presume that 100% of your premiums will earn the minimum guaranteed rate. Instead, the annuity company may credit only a percentage of your premiums paid for this purpose. Some contracts credit interest against only 90% or 80% of the principal amount.

Furthermore, the EIA contract may give the annuity company flexibility to change its crediting rates; however, most contracts specify certain minimum crediting rates that the annuity company must follow. You must understand how the annuity company credits your premiums paid for purposes of calculating interest payments, and the limitations on the annuity company to change these calculations within a product.

Whether a particular EIA calculates interest as simple interest or compounded interest can make a dramatic difference in the rate of return ultimately paid. This is something that will be set forth in the contract, and requires a clear understanding of the contract terms and the effect of simple versus compounded interest.[9] You may be better off with a lower interest rate that is compounded than a higher interest rate that is simple.

---

8. Again, many EIAs allow small "free withdrawals" to be made during the surrender penalty without charges being incurred. Some products with annual reset (ratchet) index-linking methods may allow for an annual lock-in of profits such that free withdrawals can be made from the product without negative consequences. Note, however, that any withdrawals that are made will not earn future interest, and any withdrawals made prior to the annuitant reaching age 59½ may trigger the 10% early distribution penalty for income tax purposes.

Bonuses

An increasing number of EIA contracts now pay a *premium bonus* that is usually credited to the contract in the first year. This bonus effectively increases the value of the EIA, and all subsequent Interest Crediting and Index Crediting will usually be measured against this increased value. The best way to look at the bonus is that your EIA is up that much immediately, and in the worst case during the term of the contract you will at least get the bonus amount plus any interest crediting.

For example, assume that you put $100,000 into an EIA, which features a one-time immediate bonus of 5%. This means that from the start of the contract, subsequent growth (whether interest rate or index rate) will be from $105,000 instead of $100,000.

Bonuses are offered as incentives to induce the purchases of EIAs into the contracts that offer them. But financially there is no "free lunch" and the EIAs that offer bonuses may not be as attractive with their interest rates, index rates, or participation rates as EIAs that do not offer bonuses. It is important that your agent illustrate the possible performance of EIAs that have bonuses against similar EIAs that do not.

Some agents will offer EIAs with bonuses as an incentive to create some "immediate cash" available for immediate withdrawal and use by the consumer.[10]

---

9. What the NASD says (see Appendix A)
    The way that an annuity company calculates interest earned during the term of an EIA can make a big difference in the amount of money you will earn. Some EIAs pay simple interest during the term of the annuity. Because there is no compounding of interest, your return will be lower.
    What the NAIC says (see Appendix B)
    Some annuities pay simple interest during an index term. That means index-linked interest is added to your original premium amount but does not compound during the term. Others pay compound interest during a term, which means that index-linked interest that has already been credited also earns interest in the future. In either case, however, the interest earned in one term is usually compounded in the next.
    It is important for you to know whether your annuity pays compound or simple interest during a term. While you may earn less from an annuity that pays simple interest, it may have other features you want, such as a higher participation rate.
10. Bonuses are also sometimes used to solicit the early termination of an older non-EIA annuity in order to participate in the advantages of an EIA. Often the termination of those other products will result in surrender charges or taxes, for which the bonus is meant to compensate.

This is a questionable practice, insofar as without the bonus the contract will not generate as favorable growth as if the bonus were left in. One must also be warned that the 10% early distribution penalty for tax purposes could apply to the bonus if the owner has not yet reached age 59½.

It is sometimes suggested that the fact that the insurance companies offer bonuses only shows that the products are bad, and require incentives to induce purchases. While it is true that the insurance companies are trying to incentivize the purchase of its EIA, it does not follow that EIAs are bad products. Instead, any bonuses paid should simply be factored into the overall return. Bonuses can give certain EIA contracts a significant head start in performance, but a consumer should understand how any limitations on performance affect returns as compared to similar EIAs that do not offer bonuses.

3

INDEX CREDITING: THE MAXIMUM RETURN

Whereas *interest crediting* provides at least the minimum return, *index crediting* hopefully will provide the maximum return at the end of the term because it is measured in some fashion against the chosen index.[11] The traditional EIA contract was tied to only a single index (most often the S&P 500), and offered only a single method by which the contract value against the index could be determined. Some newer EIA products offer the opportunity to tie to multiple indexes, to annually change indexes, and to choose different indexing methods for calculating the contract value.

There are now many diverse methods for calculating how the market indexed credit is calculated. At the time of this writing there were over 50 identifiable methods, and the underwriters for the insurance companies are constantly

---

11. What the NAIC says (see Appendix B)

    Two features that have the greatest effect on the amount of additional interest that may be credited to an equity-indexed annuity are the indexing method and the participation rate. It is important to understand the features and how they work together.

    An equity-indexed annuity is a fixed annuity, either immediate or deferred, that earns interest or provides benefits that are linked to an external equity reference or an equity index. The value of the index might be tied to a stock or other equity index. One of the most commonly used indexes is Standard & Poor's 500 Composite Stock Price Index (the S&P 500), which is an equity index. The value of any index varies from day to day and is not predictable. When you buy an equity-indexed annuity you own an insurance contract. You are not buying shares of any stock of index.

    The indexing method means the approach used to measure the amount of change, if any, in the index. Some of the most common indexing methods, which are explained more fully later on, include annual reset (ratcheting), high-water mark and point-to-point.

dreaming up new methods in an attempt to create more attractive products. Some of these methods will be discussed in the following Chapter 4 on Indexing Methods. The returns generated by these methods may be further enhanced or limited by the contractual provisions which are discussed below.

Participation Rates

We have already discussed participation rates as a potential limitation on the base interest rates paid by the annuity company. But participation rates can also operate to limit the index-linked return.

The participation rate is something that is found in few other products besides EIAs, and therefore is poorly understood (if at all) by most consumers. The participation rate determines how much of the increase in the index will be credited to the contract. Some EIA contacts allow full participation, i.e., if the index goes up 20% then the contract is credited with a 20% rise. Other EIAs limit participation to some defined percentage, such as a 90% of the rise in the index—so that if the contact goes up 20% then the contract is credited with an 18% increase.[12]

Participation rates of less than 100% help to protect the insurance companies in some situations and may allow them to offer higher interests rates or caps. For instance, you might be better off with a product that allows you a 90% participation rate against a 9% cap (thus allowing 8.1%) as opposed to a 100% participation rate on an 8% cap. Participation rates are not a defect of EIAs and are easy to understand once they are explained, but they are simply another moving part that may limit your returns.[13]

---

12. <u>What the NASD says</u> (see Appendix A)
    A participation rate determines how much of the gain in the index will be credited to the annuity. For example, the annuity company may set the participation rate at 80%, which means the annuity would only be credited with 80% of the gain experienced by the index.
    The participation rate decides how much of the increase in the index will be used to calculate index-linked interest. For example, if the calculated change in the index is 9% and the participation rate is 70%, the index-linked interest rate for your annuity will be 6.3% (9% x 70% = 6.3%). A company may set a different participation rate for newly issued annuities as often as each day. Therefore, the initial participation rate in your annuity will depend on when it is issued by the company. The company usually guarantees the participation rate for a specific period (from one year to the entire term). When that period is over, the company sets a new participation rate for the next period. Some annuities guarantee that the participation rate will never be set lower than a specified minimum or higher than a specified maximum.

Averaging

Some EIAs will participate in the index based on *averaging* the indexed-linked returns during the entire period rather than simply subtracting the beginning point from the end point. This helps to protect the consumer in case the contract started on a high point or if the index crashed slightly before or on the end date. In other words, averaging smoothes out performance by taking out both the lows and the highs.

The downside is, of course, that some upside performance will be lost if the contract started on a low point or peaked slightly before or on the end date. You must understand whether your EIA contract participates in the index upside on strictly a beginning-end basis, or whether it is averaged periodically throughout.[14]

Caps

Many EIAs have *caps* that are limitations set on the upwards market participation of the EIA against the index.[15] For example, an annuity company may create an annual interest cap of 10% or a monthly interest cap of 3%. Caps are defined in the contract, and can substantially affect the index performance of an EIA. You

---

13. What the NAIC says (see Appendix B)

    The participation rate may vary greatly from one annuity to another and from time to time within a particular annuity. Therefore, it is important for you to know how your annuity's participation rate works with the indexing method. A high participation rate may be offset by other features, such as simple interest, averaging, or a point-to-point indexing method. On the other hand, an annuity company may offset a lower participation rate by also offering a feature such as an annual reset indexing method.

14. What the NASD says (see Appendix A)

    Some EIAs average an index's value either daily or monthly rather than use the actual value of the index on a specified date. Averaging may reduce the amount of index-linked interest you earn.

    What the NAIC says (see Appendix B)

    In some annuities, the average of an index's value is used rather than the actual value of the index on a specified date. The index averaging may occur at the beginning, the end, or throughout the entire term of the annuity.

    Averaging at the beginning of a term protects you from buying your annuity at a high point, which would reduce the amount of interest you might earn. Averaging at the end of the term protects you against severe declines in the index and losing index-linked interest as a result. On the other hand, averaging may reduce the amount of index-linked interest you earn when the index rises either near the start or at the end of the term.

simply must understand whatever caps are in your EIA contract and how they affect the performance of your EIA during its term.

Caps typically allow the annuity company to offer higher participation rates, as discussed above. Your agent should help you to decide whether you would be better off with higher caps or higher participation rates when comparing particular contracts. For instance, a 10% cap with an 80% participation rate (thus allowing a maximum 8.0% return) would not be as favorable as a 9% cap with a 90% participation rate (allowing 8.1%).

The most common caps are annual caps and monthly caps, but of course as underwriters come up with new products there will be more and different types of caps. Note that some contracts give the annuity company some leeway to change the caps as certain market conditions change. If the annuity company has such leeway, the contract will usually define boundaries so that the changes are not completely arbitrary.

Spreads, Margins and Administrative Fees

In calculating the index-linked return, some EIAs deduct a percentage from the positive change in the index. This percentage may be in addition to or in lieu of participation rates or caps, and is variously referred to as the "spread", "margin" or sometimes "administrative fee".[16]

For example, a particular EIA might charge a 2% per year spread from the index-linked return. If the term of the EIA is 10 years, and the index performed at an average of 12% per year, you could calculate that the average return would instead be 10% per year because of the 2% annual spread.

---

15. What the NASD says (see Appendix A)
    Interest Rate Caps. Some EIAs may put a cap or upper limit on your return. This cap rate in generally stated as a percentage. This is the maximum rate of interest the annuity will earn. For example, if the index linked to the annuity gained 10% and the cap rate was 8%, then the gain in the annuity would be 8%.
    What the NAIC says (see Appendix B)
    Some annuities may put an upper limit, or cap, on the index-linked interest rate. This is the maximum rate of interest the annuity will earn. Not all annuities have a cap rate.
    While a cap limits the amount of interest you might earn each year, annuities with this feature may have other product features you want, such as annual interest crediting or the ability to take partial withdrawals. Also, annuities that have a cap may have a higher participation rate.

Indexes and Dividends

Not only is an EIA's link to the market index limited by such things as participation rates and caps, but the EIA also will not receive dividends as if the stocks comprising the index had been purchased directly. EIAs are typically linked to the performance of the index (a raw statistical number), instead of the actual stocks underlying the index (which are income-producing assets). Thus, EIAs do not give credit for dividends that could have been reinvested into the companies had you held those stocks individually.[17]

Of course, if you held the stocks individually, or invested in a mutual fund that holds those stocks, you could risk the loss of your principal if the value of those stocks decline below the price you paid for them. With an EIA, you simply don't have this risk. You are trading the dividends you might have received for not having the risk of investment losses.

Most products use a simple price index for the S&P 500, instead of taking into account reinvested dividends. The difference can be as much as 3% annually. It may seem like you are getting a return as if you had invested in the stocks that comprise the index, but you will not be.

---

16. <u>The NASD says</u>
    Some EIAs use a spread, margin or asset fee in addition to, or instead of, a participation rate. This percentage will be subtracted from any gain in the index linked to the annuity. For example, if the index gained 10% and the spread/margin/asset fee is 3.5%, then the gain in the annuity would be only 6.5%.
    <u>What the NAIC says</u> (see Appendix B)
    In some annuities, the index-linked interest rate is computed by subtracting a specific percentage from any calculated change in the index. This percentage, sometimes referred to as the "margin," "spread," or "administrative fee," might be instead of, or in addition to, a participation rate. For example, if the calculated change in the index is 10%, your annuity might specify that 2.25% will be subtracted from the rate to determine the interest rate credited. In this example, the rate would be 7.75% (10%-2.25% = 7.75%). In this example, the company subtracts the percentage only if the change in the index produces a positive interest rate.
17. <u>What the NASD says</u> (see Appendix A)
    Most EIAs only count equity index gains from market price changes, excluding any gains from dividends. Since you're not earning dividends, you won't earn as much as if you invested directly in the market.
    <u>What the NAIC says</u> (see Appendix B)
    Depending on the index used, stock dividends may or may not be included in the index's value. For example, the S&P 500 is a stock price index and only considers the prices of stocks. It does not recognize any dividends paid on those stocks.

Is the difference between the index and the index with reinvested dividends significant over many years? You bet. But a deal killer? Usually not.

The reason it is not a deal killer is that even without reinvested dividends, most indexes still perform pretty well over the long term and usually much better than CD or bond rates, which is why you want the potential to take some of the upside of the indexes. As long as you understand that you will not be receiving or reinvesting dividends, it may not make a significant difference in your purchase decision.[18]

Once again, this is a question of suitability and risk: If you can stomach the risk of the index going down and possible loss of principal, then you should not be purchasing EIAs. You should instead be buying the stocks that comprise the index itself and the broader markets where the total return will be higher because of both the dividends paid and the ability to fully participate in the index's rises (and falls) without a limiting formula. If you cannot stomach this risk, then trading off the upside market potential for the benefit of total downside market protection by way of an EIA is for you.

Be Careful of "Backtested" Returns

If you hear that an EIA was *backtested*, it means that the EIA was tested against historical returns, such as those from the last 20 years. Beware that backtesting is certainly no guarantee of future performance. To the contrary, the financial markets move in an unpredictable and random fashion and are significantly affected by abnormal events such as terrorism and petroleum shortages. There is also a risk that those who designed the EIA did so in a way that would make it look good in backtesting during a particular period.

Backtesting can help to illustrate the importance of certain *moving parts* (terms that can change) of the annuity, as well as the effect of caps and participation rates in "real time". But it really is more for the use of the agent in understanding the product than as a sales tool for potential EIA consumers. For illustrations to clients, the use of *Monte Carlo analysis* (which utilizes repeated samplings of totally random hypothetical market returns) may present a more accurate picture of likely returns for a given product.

---

18. It can be argued that the loss of reinvested dividends is made up for by annual reset (ratchet) annuities that credit the index return with only a zero in negative years.

4
INDEXING METHODS

The formula by which your EIA contract will calculate its return against the index to which it is linked is known as the *indexing method*.[19] Currently, there are over 50 indexing methods and newer methods are being developed by annuity company underwriters in order to be able to offer new and more attractive products to consumers. Any attempt to describe or catalogue each of these new methods, or to anticipate new methods, is simply beyond the scope of this book.

Buyers of EIAs—and sometimes agents too—often agonize over trying to pick the "best" method, based on how they hope the stock markets will perform. But there is no "best" indexing method. Which method works best for you will depend on future market performance over the term of the EIA.

The problem is: Armed with the most sophisticated financial modeling tools, financial analysts have great difficulty in accurately predicting market behavior just two or three years in the future. You cannot possibly know in advance how the markets will perform during the term of your EIA, which will be from at least seven to maybe as long as 14 years into the future.

Because it cannot be known in advance which indexing method will work best, it is suggested that at least two different indexing methods be used, and hopefully as many different indexing methods as practical. The more methods

---

19. <u>What the NAIC says</u> (see Appendix B)

    An equity-indexed annuity is different from other fixed annuities because of the way it credits interest to your annuity's value. Some fixed annuities only credit interest calculated at a rate set in the contract. Other fixed annuities also credit interest at rates set from time to time by the annuity company. Equity-indexed annuities credit interest using a formula based on changes in the index to which the annuity is linked. The formula decides how the additional interest, if any, is calculated and credited. How much additional interest you get and when you get it depends on the features of your particular annuity.

that you use, the more likely it is that you will obtain an average performance between methods.

To achieve such diversification the consumer may be required to purchase more than one EIA. That has the additional advantage of allowing the consumer to diversify among EIA companies as well (and thus further mitigate the very small risk of annuity company failure).

Some indexing methods will work best under some market conditions, and other will work best under other market conditions. For instance, if the markets perform very well in the first few years, but poorly in later years, then the annual reset (ratchet) method might yield the best return. By contrast, if the markets make steady gains during the period of the contract with few or no loss years, then a point-to-point method might yield the best return.

Many new EIAs allow for several indexing methods, which can be changed on certain dates, such as annual contract anniversary dates. These EIAs may also allow consumers to use several of the indexing methods at the same time within the contract, thus allowing the consumer to purchase one contract instead of several.

There is one practical difference between index methods: When you know what your returns are. Some methods have "reset" features that lock in gains on some periodic basis, usually annually. With these methods, you can see exactly how your EIA has performed during that period. By contrast, other EIAs will not measure their indexed return until the EIA has run its full term. So, if you need to know what interest has been credited at a particular point in time, you will want to choose a reset product.

Annual Reset

One common method typically looks at the index at the end of each contact anniversary date, and locks in gains made as of that date. This method is known as the *annual reset* method, or sometimes as the *ratchet* method. Even if the index later goes down, the gains that have already been made will not be lost.[20]

If the index has declined from the previous anniversary, there is no downward adjustment and the contract simply credits zero for the period. For example, if the index performs at–6.3% during the period, the credit percentage for the period will be 0.0%. This means that the indexed value can only go up. The previous period's end value for the index (not the annuity value) is then used as the starting point for the new period, so that each period is looked at in isolation to all other periods and without regard to what gains were made before.

The attractiveness of the annual reset method is that no matter what happens in subsequent years, you will have locked in gains and your profits will not be lost. This is the method that you would want to use if the stock market makes steady but slow gains, and you don't want to lose those gains if there is a crash or prolonged bear market.

The disadvantage of the annual reset method is that it will usually have caps that will limit your upside market potential. For example, an annuity with an annual reset may have a 7% cap. If the index has increased 21% on a contract anniversary date, then your EIA would participate in only a 7% maximum increase for that year. You would not use this method if you expected the stock market to have only a few spectacular years, with the other years being stagnant or negative. Note that while the caps will limit upside potential, this may be more than offset by the fact that negative years will be recorded simply as zeros and no value will be lost.

High Water Mark

The *High Water Mark* method compares the index at various periods during the contract, most typically on the contract anniversaries, to the index level at the start of the term.[21] For example, let's say the index has increased by 17% by year 3, by 54% by year 5, but by year 7 has declined to 36%, and at the end of the

---

20. What the NASD says (see Appendix A)
    Annual Reset (Rachet): Compares the change in the index from the beginning to the end of each year. Any declines are ignored.
    Advantage: Your gain is "locked in" each year.
    Disadvantage: Can be combined with other features, such as lower cap rates and participation rates that will limit the amount of interest you might gain each year.
    What the NAIC says (see Appendix B)
    Annual Reset: Index-linked interest, if any, is determined each year by comparing the index value at the end of the contract year with the index value at the start of the contract year. Interest is added to your annuity each year during the term.
    Features. Since the interest earned is "locked in" annually and the index value is "reset" at the end of each year, future decreases in the index will not affect the interest you have already earned. Therefore, your annuity using the annual reset method may credit more interest than annuities using other methods when the index fluctuates up and down often during the term. This design is more likely than others to give you access to index-linked interest before the term ends.
    Trade-Offs. Your annuity's participation rate may change each year and generally will be lower than that of other indexing methods. Also an annual reset design may use a cap or averaging to limit the total amount of interest you might earn each year.

term the index is only up a total of 43%. With the High Water Mark method, the contract value would be calculated against the highest point on an anniversary date, in this case the 54% in year 5.

Without participation rates and caps, this method would probably give you the highest risk-adjusted returns of any indexing method. However, where the High Water Mark method is used, it is often combined with participation rates less than 100% and often significant caps. Also be aware that only highs reached at the periods where the comparisons occur are counted. If these periods are the anniversary date of the contract, this means that any highs reached between these periods will not be counted.

---

21. What the NASD says (see Appendix A)
    High Water Mark—Looks at the index value at various points during the contract, usually annual anniversaries. It then takes the highest of these values and compares it to the index level at the start of the term.
    Advantage: May credit you with more interest than other indexing methods and protect against declines in the index.
    Disadvantage: Because interest is not credited until the end of the term, you may not receive any index-link gain if you surrender your EIA early. It can also be combined with other features; such as lower cap rates and participation rates that will limit the amount of interest you might gain each year.
    What the NAIC says (see Appendix B)
    High-Water Mark: The index-linked interest, if any, is decided by looking at the index value at various points during the term, usually the annual anniversaries of the date you bought the annuity. The interest is based on the difference between the highest index value and the index value at the start of the term. Interest is added to your annuity at the end of the term.
    Features. Since interest is calculated using the highest value of the index on a contract anniversary during the term, this design may credit higher interest than some other designs if the index reaches a high point early or in the middle of the term, then drops off at the end of the term.
    Trade-Offs. Interest is not credited until the end of the term. In some annuities, if you surrender your annuity before the end of the term, you may not get index-linked interest for that term. In other annuities, you may receive index-linked interest, based on the highest anniversary value to date and the annuity's vesting schedule. Also, contracts with this design may have a lower participation rate than annuities using other designs or may use a cap to limit the total amount of interest you might earn.

Point-to-Point

The *Point-to-Point* method usually credits the contract with some value based upon the value of the index at some specific date, such as at the end of the contract term, with regard to any highs or lows that were reached in the interim. This method often offers the fullest participation in the index, but index highs are not locked in, and it risks a serious decline of the index's value immediately prior to the time the point is measured.[22]

This method is probably best for the longest-term EIAs, since it can be anticipated that over long periods the index will "regress to the mean" and approximate its historical returns. Another way of saying this is that within the markets "time heals all wounds" and that interim performance is irrelevant over a long period of time, so long as the index follows its normal upwards trend. Because of this effect, the Point-to-Point method should probably be used with your EIAs that have the longest terms.

Some Point-to-Point contracts charge a spread, such as 2% per year, while others may limit participation to less than 100% or impose caps. The contract may also limit or alter the way the means of crediting based on Point-to-Point. For instance, a contract may not give the full increase in value based on the end point, but may instead use the end point to average the index over the term of the contact, and credit interest on a compounded basis based on that average rate,

---

22. <u>What the NASD says</u> (see Appendix A)

  Point-to-Point—Compares the change in the index at two discrete points in time, such as the beginning and ending dates of the contract term.

  Advantage: May be combined with other features, such as higher cap and participation rates, that may credit you with more interest.

  Disadvantage: Relies on single point in time to calculate interest. Therefore, even if the index that your annuity is linked to is going up throughout the term of your investment, if it declines dramatically on the last day of the term, then part or all of the earlier gain can be lost. Because interest is not credited until the end of the term, you may not receive any index-link gain if you surrender your EIA early.

  <u>What the NAIC says</u> (see Appendix B)

  Point-to-Point: The index-linked interest, if any, is based on the *difference* between the index value at the end of the term and the index value at the start of the term. Interest is added to your annuity at the end of the term.

  Features. Since interest cannot be calculated before the end of the term, use of this design may permit a higher participation rate than annuities using other designs.

  Trade-Offs. Since interest is not credited until the end of the term, typically six or seven years, you may not be able to get the index-linked interest until the end of the term.

less some percentage defined in the contract, say 2% per year. You must carefully review the contract to understand these limitations.

While Point-to-Point contracts offer the potential for the best long-term returns, they have the disadvantage that you cannot gauge the contract performance until the end of the term. Until the final point is reached, the growth will appear to be 0.0% even if the market is sharply up. Those who feel that they need to know the value of their EIA during the term for planning purposes may not prefer this method.[23]

Diversify Your Methods

So what is the best method? Nobody knows in advance, since what will later turn out to be the best method depends on how the markets perform. Some methods will do better in volatile markets, while others will do better in steady markets. The truth is that whichever method you choose will have similar performance to all other methods.

Your choice of methods is not nearly as important as choosing a quality company or finding products with the highest minimum interest rates, participation rates, caps, and other features. Despite this, buyers of EIAs seem to struggle over the choice of method, though this is really just blind-guessing as to how the markets might perform over the long term.

As mentioned earlier, your best strategy is to buy several different products and diversify the methods so you can get the best average performance over time. Since perhaps the most important consideration is the strength of the annuity company, you should be diversifying your purchase of EIAs among several annuity companies anyway. When you do this, you should take the opportunity to diversify your indexing methods as well.

---

23. Most Point-to-Point contracts treat the death of the annuitant as the end of the term for purposes of measuring contract performance as of that date.

5

PAYOUT METHODS

We have discussed how an EIA accumulates money, and now it is time to discuss how an EIA distributes money to you. Most annuities are not used for making payments, but instead are used as a vehicle to accumulate funds which are then simply withdrawn against the policy value or the EIA is exchanged tax-free for another annuity and the accumulation process starts anew.

Annuity Stream

The main purpose of an annuity is to provide payments until you die, such as to provide your post-retirement income needs. If you elect to *annuitize* your EIA, this will cause the regular payments to begin. Most EIAs will allow you to vary the frequency and amount of your payouts to meet your particular needs.[24]

Other than surrender charges, the only real limitation on how payments can be made to you relates to taxes. As we have previously discussed, payouts will usually need to begin after age 59½ to avoid the 10% tax for early distribution from a tax-deferred annuity. See Chapter 9 on Taxes.

---

24. <u>What the NAIC says</u> (see Appendix B)

   One of the most important benefits of deferred annuities is the right to use the value built up during the accumulation period to provide income payments during the payout period. While income payments are usually made monthly, you can often choose more or less frequent payments. The size of income payments is based on both the accumulated value in your annuity and the annuity's "benefit rate" that is in effect when income payments begin. The insurance company uses the benefits rate to compute the amount of income payment it will pay you for each $1,000 of accumulated value in your annuity. The benefit rate usually depends on your age and sex, and the form of annuity payment you have chosen. You can usually choose from many forms of annuity payments. You might choose payments that continue as long as you live, or as long as either you or your spouse live, or payments that continue for a set number of years.

Tax-Free Exchanges

As mentioned, most EIAs are never annuitized but are simply exchanged for another annuity at the end of the term. In general, you are allowed to exchange one annuity for another without triggering taxes under section 1035 of the Internal Revenue Code. This is known as a *1035 Exchange*.

The annuity that you trade for does not typically have to be the same type as your existing annuity. You may trade one EIA for a different type of EIA (or several different types), such as a variable annuity, a true fixed annuity, or other type of annuity, typically without triggering any taxes.[25] You can also make a tax-free exchange of a life insurance policy for an annuity, but you cannot make a tax-free exchange of an annuity for a life insurance policy. That door only swings one way.

The Death Benefit

But what if you die before you get all your money back? Most EIAs typically provide some form of benefit upon the death of the annuitant, usually the greater of the guaranteed minimum rate or the index-linked rate.[26] The person who receives the death benefit (if there is one) is known as the *beneficiary*.

The death benefit is a minimal benefit which usually just assures the return of the contract value to heirs; it is not meant to be a replacement or substitute for life insurance, and probably will serve that role poorly if at all. As discussed in Chapter 9 which relates to Tax Considerations, annuities are generally inefficient estate planning tools unless placed into a specially designed trust structure.

Life Only, No Refund

With this payout type, no matter how long you live you would receive guaranteed payments for life. But at your death, no money would be paid to beneficiaries even if you died right after the first payment.

Very simply, if you live past your life expectancy then you win and the annuity company loses, but if you die early then the annuity company wins and your

---

25. You may also be able to exchange other retirement assets for an EIA. Contact your financial planner or tax planner for more information and advice on how to make such an exchange without triggering unnecessary tax consequences.
26. What the NAIC says (see Appendix B)
    Annuities provide a variety of death benefits. The most common death benefit is either the guaranteed minimum value or the value determined by the index-linked formula.

heirs lose. Because the annuity company does not have to guarantee any minimum benefits to your heirs, you will typically get the highest annuity payouts with this option.

Life Annuity, Period Certain

With this payout type, you would also receive guaranteed payments for life no matter how long you live. However, if you died within a certain period of time, say, 10 years, your heirs would receive at least the amount of any premium payments less the amount of any annuity payments made to you. After 10 years that guarantee would go away and the heirs would receive nothing. Depending on the contract, beneficiaries would receive either a lump sum distribution or installment payments spread over a period of years. Because of the guarantee during the period, the payout would be less than the Life Only payout type.

Joint and Last Survivor

There are basically two annuitants with this type of payout, which allows the surviving spouse to continue to receive payments until their death. Some joint and survivor contracts reduce the amount of payout on the first death, while other contracts will give a refund to heirs if both spouses die within a certain period.

Mandatory Annuitization

The vast majority of EIAs allow you to take cash out of the annuity at the end of the term or allow you to roll the annuity over into another annuity or other financial product. This is very important because it allows you the option to continue to defer the taxes on this money. However, a few EIAs will require you to annuitize at the end of the term and start taking the guaranteed payments whether you want them or not. This is a very unfortunate and significant restriction, and you should absolutely not purchase one of these EIAs unless you absolutely know for a certainty that you will want to annuitize it at the end of the term.

6

THE ANNUITY COMPANY

If you hold an EIA past the surrender period without making any withdrawals, the only way to lose money is for the annuity company that issued the EIA to become insolvent. Thus, your most important decision in choosing a particular EIA may be the financial strength of the annuity company that issues it.[27]

Historically, annuity companies have only very rarely failed—and much more rarely than the corporate businesses into which equity investments are normally made. Indeed, annuity company failures are so rare that the possible insolvency of the annuity company is almost never mentioned by critics of EIAs as a reason not to buy one. As of the date of this writing, no EIA consumer has ever lost a cent because of annuity company insolvency.

Although EIAs are not as safe as government bonds or government-backed instruments, they are much safer than even "blue chip" securities, and even highly rated corporate bonds. EIAs are roughly comparable in their safety to money-market funds, which are usually not protected by FDIC but instead are backed by the bank's reserves and other assets.

Unlike variable annuities, EIAs are not backed by segregated reserves or specific assets. As the owner of an EIA, you will not own the index, index shares, or the stocks comprising the index. Instead, you will own a contract whereby the annuity company promises to pay you money in the future from its general assets. EIAs are thus backed by all of the assets of the annuity company generally, and not just specific assets or pools of assets. Because of this, the financial strength of the annuity company is of overwhelming importance.

The laws of each state require annuity companies to keep large reserves and other assets available to satisfy their obligations. These laws are enforced by the

---

27. What the NASD says (see Appendix A)
    Your guaranteed return is only as good as the annuity company that gives it. While it is not a common occurrence that a life annuity company is unable to meet its obligations, it happens.

state insurance commissioners, who annually send out teams of auditors to the annuity companies to verify their solvency and financial strength to meet their obligations. On top of that, each state has a "guarantee fund" or something similar available to help bail out insolvent insurers. So, even in the rare event of an annuity company failure, it is likely you would get back a substantial proportion of your premium payments.

Nonetheless, annuity company insolvency is always a possibility, so some degree of additional safety can be gained by diversification. By purchasing several smaller contracts from several different annuity companies, instead of one large contract from a single annuity company, you greatly diminish the already slight risk of losing money because of annuity company failure.

Measuring Financial Strength

The financial strength of an annuity company is ordinarily evaluated by a ratings service that pours through the annuity company's balance sheets and inspects assets to come up with *annuity company ratings* that give an indication of financial strength.

Annuity company ratings are routinely published, and the insurance agent who offers you the EIA is required to provide you with current rating information. You will want to purchase your EIA from an annuity company rated at least BBB or B + +. Since the financial strength of the annuity company is the most important factor in purchasing EIAs, you should seriously consider accepting a product with a lower payout from a higher rated company, such as from carrier rated at least AA or A+ or better, rather than a product offering a slightly higher return from a lower rated company.

Diversification of Annuity Companies

While annuity company insolvency presents only a miniscule risk of loss, even that can be mitigated simply by spreading out the purchase of EIAs among several annuity companies instead of just one. As discussed in Chapter 4 which discusses Indexing Methods, if you are placing a large amount of money into EIAs you will want to diversify among types of EIA products anyway so as to have the greatest of chance of gains, and in doing so you might as well diversify among annuity companies too. By purchasing several contracts from several different annuity companies, you greatly diminish the already minimal risk of losing money because of the possible failure of one of the companies.

Reputation Regarding Moving Parts

All EIAs have one or more "moving parts" which are terms that the annuity company may arbitrarily change so as to financially protect itself in adverse market conditions. An annuity company could, as an example, retain the ability to change participation rates or caps at its discretion. This helps to protect the insurance company in adverse market conditions, but of course it also may limit your returns.

For instance, an EIA has a minimum guaranteed interest rate that will be paid, but the annuity company could pay a higher interest rate to attract consumers. While the annuity company is not required to pay the higher rate, and could at any time simply go back to the minimum guaranteed interest rate, it has a marketing incentive not to do so.

You should talk with your agent regarding the annuity company's reputation for changing terms in mid-stream. An annuity company that regularly changes terms to the detriment of its consumers should be avoided, and one that tries to benefit its consumers should be preferred.

7

SUITABILITY ISSUES: COMPLEXITY, DISCLOSURE, LIQUIDITY AND WITHDRAWALS

Some advocates of EIAs would argue that there are no inherently "bad" EIAs, but only that particular EIAs are sold to persons for whom they are not suitable. As discussed throughout this book, suitability is one of the most important issues for a consumer.

While questions of suitability for a particular consumer must be resolved by an overall facts-and-circumstances analysis of their individual financial needs, risk tolerance, and similar considerations, there are a few bright line situations where EIAs are patently unsuitable.[28]

First, if you anticipate needing large withdrawals[29] from an EIA during the surrender period, then an EIA is unsuitable for you. For this purpose, your liquidity should be conservatively analyzed and the "worst case" position taken. Do not presume that liquidity will be available from growth of your investments or increases in home equity, etc. Very simply, if you will not have sufficient liquidity to meet your liquidity needs outside of the EIA, then the EIA is unsuitable for you, and you should stick with cash & equivalents even if their return is lower. See *Liquidity, Early Withdrawals & Loss of Principal*, below.

Second, if the EIA is purchased purely as a vehicle to pass wealth to your children, and you will not require the cash after the contract date, then you might be better off purchasing a life insurance policy—preferably, after engaging in estate planning so that the policy is held outside of your estate.

Third, even with guidance from your insurance agent or financial advisor you are unable to grasp the basic operations of an EIA, then it is not for you. See *Complexity and Disclosure*, below.

SUITABILITY ISSUES: COMPLEXITY, DISCLOSURE, LIQUIDITY AND WITHDRAWALS

Fourth, not all of your long-term money should be placed into EIAs. You should instead keep some significant portion of your money available for investment into the equity markets to more efficiently hedge against the possibility of long-term inflation. Like any long-term purchase, EIAs should only be purchased as part of a thoroughly considered financial plan.

Complexity and Disclosure

Some critics complain that EIAs are extremely complex so that the ordinary consumer has little chance of fully understanding them or their myriad terms and conditions. To some degree, this is a valid criticism. Indeed, it seems that not even all agents who sell EIAs completely understand all their variables and terms.

EIAs are very complex financial products that are sometimes difficult for even experienced investment advisors to figure out. Avoid those who describe EIAs as "simple" products. The concept may be simple, but the contract terms are not.

The complexity of EIA contracts sometimes forces the agent to basically tell the client *"Trust Me"* as to how the product will work in particular circumstances. It is here that many of the most common problems with EIAs arise, because the agent many not fully understand how the product works, the agent may inno-

---

28. <u>What the NAIC says</u> (see Appendix B)

    As with any other insurance product, you must carefully consider your own personal situation and how you feel about the choices available. No single annuity design may have all the features you want. It is important to understand the features and trade-offs available so you can choose the annuity that is right for you. Keep in mind that it may be misleading to compare one annuity to another unless you compare all the other features of each annuity. You must decide for yourself what combination of features makes the most sense for you. Also, remember that it is not possible to predict the future market behavior of an index.

    The questions listed below may help you decide which type of annuity, if any, meets your retirement planning and financial needs. You should consider what your goals are for the money you may put into the annuity. You need to think about how much risk you're willing to take with the money. Ask yourself:
    - How long can I leave my money in the annuity?
    - What do I expect to use the money for in the future?
    - Am I interested in a variable annuity with the potential for higher earnings that are not guaranteed and willing to risk losing the principal?
    - Is a guaranteed interest rate more important to me, with little or no risk of losing the principal?
    - Or, am I somewhere in between these two extremes and willing to take some risks?

cently misrepresent how the product works, the consumer may misunderstand how the product works, and in rare cases the agent may even take advantage of the complexity to intentionally deceive the consumer about how the product works.

At the same time, complexity is not *ipso facto* bad and the mere fact that the contracts are complex does not affect their performance. You may not fully understand how the electronic ignition in your car works, but that probably doesn't keep you from driving. EIAs are the same way—you may never understand completely how they work, but you will need to know at least the basics so that you can operate them safely.

There is nothing wrong with a good advisor who fully understands EIAs and individual products simplifying for you how a particular EIA might work. For most consumers, the decision to purchase an EIA will often come down to two or three primary issues—but this doesn't mean that the complexity of these products or their contractual qualifications and limitations can be safely ignored.

The *Trust Me* factor also highlights the critical importance of having a good and honest advisor evaluate and choose the right EIA for a particular consumer, and to fully explain in plain English (as opposed to legalese) how the products work.

For the same reason, disreputable agents who sell EIAs—and particularly those who direct-market them as a cure for every financial ill—should be avoided. Likewise, agents who attempt to oversimplify or gloss over important aspects of how a particular EIA works should be avoided. Buying an EIA is an important decision; find a good agent to assist you.

Complexity may be an issue as it relates to suitability. A person lacking the business acumen or experience to gain at least a basic understanding of how these products work, with the assistance of their advisor or agent, is ordinarily not a suitable prospect to purchase an EIA. In other words, some people will never adequately understand EIAs and how they work, and these people should never purchase them unless they are content with the minimum return.

---

29. Meaning withdrawals in excess of any "free withdrawals" that the contract may allow you to take without any surrender penalties being incurred.

Liquidity, Early Withdrawals & Loss of Principal

Critics point out that EIAs lack liquidity, and that a large[30] early withdrawal will likely result in a loss of principal—so therefore it is theoretically possible for an EIA to lose money.[31] Also, EIAs usually have surrender charges that can dramatically reduce the returns paid if surrender is made.[32]

Admittedly, the biggest downside to an EIA is that they have significant surrender charges, especially during the first few years. Surrender charges aid the annuity company by allowing it to make long term investments of its reserves and surplus, and thus the annuity company can offer better long term returns. The contracts that promise the best long-term results may have surrender charges lasting many years. But what this means to a consumer is that they should not place their money into an EIA if they may need it during the surrender period.

This really isn't a question about liquidity, but about suitability, *i.e.*, whether an EIA is right for you. Fundamentally, EIAs are only suitable for people who will not need liquidity or withdrawals during the contract period. EIAs should, therefore, *never* be sold to or purchased by anybody who knows that they will need to access their principal before the contract period ends. Because of this, the whole liquidity and early withdrawal issue should never adversely affect the appropriately qualified consumer. It only affects those who should never have bought the EIA in the first place.

Some EIAs create additional liquidity for things such as medical emergencies. However, if this is a significant concern for a particular consumer it may mean that they cannot stomach the loss of liquidity and shouldn't be in EIAs in the first

---

30. Many EIA contracts allow for at least small, limited "free withdrawals" each year, even during the surrender period.
31. <u>What the NASD says</u> (see Appendix A)

    The guaranteed minimum return for an EIA is typically 90% of the premium paid at a 3% annual interest rate. However, if you surrender your EIA early, you may have to pay a significant surrender charge and a 10% tax penalty that will reduce or eliminate any return.

    Is it possible to lose money in an EIA? Yes. Many insurance companies only guarantee that you'll receive 90% of the premiums you paid, plus at least 3% interest. Therefore, if you don't receive any index-linked interest, you could lose money on your investment. One way that you could not receive any index-linked interest is if the index linked to your annuity declines. The other way you may not receive any index-linked interest is if you surrender your EIA before maturity. Some insurance companies will not credit you with index-linked interest when you surrender your annuity early.

place. Before consumers can consider themselves suitable for purchasing an EIA, they should have other assets and liquidity available for emergencies such as these.

Lockboxing

In some circumstances, an EIA's lack of liquidity might be beneficial since the lack of liquidity prevents or deters the consumer from attempting to access the cash prior to the end of the contract. This is known as *Lockboxing*.

---

32. <u>What the NAIC says</u> (see Appendix B)

In most cases, you can take all or part of the money out of a deferred annuity at any time during the term. There may be a cost if you do. Sometimes the cost is a stated dollar amount. In other cases, you give up index-linked interest on the amount withdrawn. Some annuities do not let you make a partial withdrawal until the end of a term.

If you withdraw all or part of the value in your annuity before the end of the term, a *withdrawal or surrender charge* may be applied. A withdrawal charge is usually a percentage of the amount being withdrawn. The percentage may be reduced or eliminated after the annuity has been in force for a certain number of years. Sometimes the charge is a reduction in the interest rate credited to the annuity.

Some annuities credit none of the index-linked interest or only part of it if you take out all your money before the end of the term. The percentage that is vested, or credited, generally increases as the term comes closer to its end and is always 100% at the end of the term.

Your annuity may have a limited "free withdrawal" provision. This lets you make one or more withdrawals without charge each year. The size of the free withdrawal is limited to a set percentage of your annuity's guaranteed or accumulated value. If you make a larger withdrawal, you may pay withdrawal charges.

You may also lose index-linked interest on amounts you withdraw. Most annuities waive withdrawal charges on withdrawals made within a set number of days at the end of each term. Some annuities waive withdrawal charges if you are confined to a nursing home or diagnosed with a terminal illness. You may, however, lose index-linked interest on withdrawals.

The index term is the period over which index-linked interest is calculated. In most product designs, interest is credited to your annuity at the end of a term. Terms are generally from one to ten years, with six or seven years being most common. Some annuities offer single terms while others offer multiple, consecutive terms. If your annuity has multiple terms, there will usually be a window at the end of each term, typically 30 days, during which you may withdraw your money without penalty. For installment premium annuities, the payment of each premium may begin a new term for that premium.

EIAs can be a good purchase for those who lack the appropriate discipline to invest in the markets, i.e., who routinely make bad investments on a whim or thinking they have a "great tip", or who lack the discipline to recognize and avoid stock market bubbles.

EIAs can also be a good purchase for those who have received a large amount of cash, such as from the sale of a business, an inheritance, or a lottery winning, and who might be tempted by risky and unfortunate business opportunities. In this case, the EIA works to protect and delay the access to the cash, hopefully to a future period where the unforeseen money will not be burning a hole in the pocket of the consumer.

For those who have made dramatic gains in the stock market, EIAs offer the opportunity to take chips off the table but still earn acceptable returns without downside market risk.

EIAs can also serve an asset protection role, since their illiquidity prior to the end of the contract will make them a much less attractive target of creditors, as opposed to bonds, stocks or mutual funds shares that can simply be attached by creditors and sold at then-current market value. If in the interim the consumer has established residency in one of the several states that protect the annuity payments, it is possible that a creditor would not be able to ever get at the annuity payments, *i.e.*, the protection becomes absolute. See Chapter 10 relating to Asset Protection.

8

PORTFOLIO ROLE OF EIAS

Equity-Indexed Annuities should typically only be purchased as part of a comprehensive financial plan that takes into consideration your overall financial needs and goals. Decisions regarding EIAs are best made as part of a comprehensive *asset allocation analysis* that intelligently divides your wealth into certain asset classes based on when you will require the money, the returns that you need to meet your goals, and the investment risks that you are comfortably willing to accept.

From a safety standpoint, EIAs can be classified with cash and equivalents such as Certificates of Deposit and money market accounts. This is because EIAs are fundamentally a fixed annuity, and the risk is very small that you will not receive at least the minimum return. But as with these other products, your risk is not that you will lose your money but that you will not earn as high returns as you might earn from more risky equity investments.

As a fixed annuity, the EIA provides that an "absolute return" will be there for you on a specific date, no matter what else happens. EIAs are thus suitable products for specific needs at specific times, usually for needs arising at least seven years in the future.

EIAs are absolutely not suitable for those who anticipate the need to access their principal prior their payout date. The reason is that EIAs are typically illiquid, and even when they do allow some limited liquidity, they are usually inefficient if early withdrawals of principal are made. So, you should never rely on accessing your principal in an EIA prior to its payout date. Some EIAs end the surrender charges as early as seven years from the date of purchase, so if you have one of these annuities, you can count on your principal being there for you only starting in year seven. However, if you buy such a product, then you will know with considerable certainty that at least your principal will be available for you starting on that date.

Because of this, EIAs are often laddered to provide for income needs for years seven to twenty from the purchase date. For example, a first EIA could be structured so that its value would become available in year seven and providing enough income for years 7 to 9, a second EIA could be structured to be available in year ten and providing enough income for years 10 to 13, and a third EIA could be structured to be available in year 14 and providing enough income for years 14 to 20.

In this case, you would know that you would have at least the minimum returns available on years 7, 10 and 14 that will take care of you from years 7 to 20. But, during that time that you know that the absolute returns will be there for you, if the index substantially increases then you will have a chance to participate in the market upside as well.

Past twenty years, the best solution is to participate in the financial markets via an asset allocated portfolio. The statistical odds are that if you hold equity investments for twenty years or longer that even with short-term booms and crashes you will begin to approach the long term averages for the respective index that you are tracking. An EIA can get some of your money past the initial period where short term market adversities can dramatically impact the mid-term returns that you anticipate having a need to access.

Sometimes, advisors will use an EIA to provide for current income during the contract period by accessing the growth of cash value within the contract. As long as appropriate types of EIAs are used for this purpose, there probably is no disadvantage to such as strategy, with the caveat that the plan should not anticipate significant withdrawal of principal prior to the end of the contract.

Compared to Cash, Money Market Funds and Certificates of Deposits

While EIAs should be classified with cash and cash-equivalents because of their high level of safety and no risk of loss due to market conditions, they usually offer several advantages.

First, some EIAs offer a minimum interest rate that can be comparable to that offered by simple CDs and money market accounts. Second, the interest earned by EIAs is tax-deferred. If the taxes are "timed" so that the EIA payments are taken at a time when you are in a lower tax bracket, this can make the post-tax returns of EIAs substantially higher than CDs and money market accounts that are immediately taxed on their interest income. Third, EIAs offer the chance for equity-like participation in the stock market according to the index linking feature, which of course no CD or money market account offers. This latter feature allows EIAs the potential to better hedge against inflation.

Because of these advantages, it is difficult to imagine why anybody would buy CDs or money market funds if they did not anticipate needing the funds during the surrender period of the EIA. Unfortunately, many people keep too much money in CDs and money market accounts with minimal interest rates, current taxes paid on the interest, and no chance of higher returns.

Compared to Medium-Term Bonds

Sometimes EIAs are compared to bonds that will pay out at roughly the same time as when the surrender charges for an EIA expire. Indeed, the investment yields for bonds and EIAs are often similar. There are important differences, however.

One difference is that bonds have complete liquidity, since you can sell them at any time. EIAs at best have limited liquidity and premature withdrawals can substantially affect their performance. So, if you think that you might need liquidity of the amount invested, you should buy the bonds. As stated repeatedly here and elsewhere, EIAs are usually unsuitable for those who might need to make withdrawals during the surrender period.

But if you don't need liquidity, EIAs are superior to bonds for several reasons: First, the value of bonds can go down if interest rates increase, meaning that you may need to hold your bonds to maturity to get your value out of them. This is because bonds are subject to market risks, such as inflation and speculation. Second, EIAs offer potential of upside if the index to which it is linked does well. Third, EIAs are tax-deferred and create opportunities to "time the tax" whereas bonds generate taxes annually and cannot be deferred.[33]

So, bonds and EIAs should not be thought of as substitutes to each other. You use bonds when you think you will need the liquidity, and you use EIAs when you know you do not. You might also buy bonds if you will need the money prior to age 59½ since EIAs are subject to the 10% early distribution penalty.

Note that EIAs should not be considered the equivalent of bonds for purposes of an asset allocation analysis. The reason is simple: Bonds can go up and down in price, and thus may have positive or negative correlations to other asset classes, whereas EIAs can only go up in value and have only positive correlations to the asset classes that overlap whichever index a particular EIA has linked itself to. In other words, you can't wait for EIAs to decline in price and then buy them cheaply as you can with bonds and most other assets.

---

33. Some types of bonds, such as municipal bonds, are effectively tax-free. But these bonds usually have relatively low returns.

Compared to Mutual Funds and Index Shares

EIAs are also sometimes compared to mutual funds, *i.e.,* funds comprised of a diverse basket of stocks. They are also sometimes compared to index shares, which are essentially stocks that track the index.

Critics of EIAs often argue that because of the ways that EIAs limit participation in returns if the index goes up, you are much better off just buying the index funds or index shares and forgetting EIAs. This is another apples-and-orangutans analysis, considering the nest egg role that EIAs are designed to play within a portfolio.

While EIAs roughly track the indexes to which they are linked subject to participation rates, caps, and other limitations, the hoped-for gains in the index should not be relied upon for planning purposes. Instead, planning which incorporates EIAs should anticipate only the minimum return, with additional growth gained because of increases in the linked index being treated much like unforeseen but welcome bonuses.

There are many differences between EIAs and mutual funds, including that mutual funds usually have many fees and expenses that can significantly drag performance. Also, the manager of a mutual fund can change or have bad luck leading to poorer results, or the existing manager can be guilty of *style drift* by taking on excessive portfolio risk in the hunt for higher returns.

Mutual funds can sometimes be very tax inefficient and can spin off significant taxes to a consumer even if the mutual fund loses money. By contrast, most EIAs have no fees or expenses and do not spin off any annual taxes as a result of portfolio turnover. Also, of course, the taxes for mutual funds are incurred immediately, but EIAs are tax deferred thus allowing the consumer to *time the tax* in many cases, such as only taking payments in retirement years when the consumer's overall tax bracket is lower.

If simply tracking the index is your goal then *index funds* and *index shares* may of course be much more efficient vehicles. An index fund is a passively-managed pool comprised of stocks in roughly the same percentage as the index, and which is designed to track the index. Index funds are very popular because of their typical low expenses and relatively low turnover and tax distributions. Very similarly, index shares are stock shares that represent a composite holding of the same shares that comprise the index. The primary advantages of index shares is that they can be traded at any time during the day when the stock market is open, just like any other stock shares, and their effective expenses and tax distributions are usually even lower than the already low index funds.

The risk with index funds and index shares is, of course, the possible loss of principal or poor long-term returns if the index declines. Mutual funds and index shares have market risk, but EIAs don't. By contrast, even if the index severely declines, EIAs will still yield their minimum return, no matter what.

9

TAX CONSIDERATIONS

Equity-Indexed Annuities are taxed just like any other fixed annuities. This mostly means that the gains accumulated in the annuity are tax-deferred during the accumulation phase, and that no tax liability will typically arise until a withdrawal is taken, payments are made, or the annuitant dies.

Tax deferral creates two significant advantages: First, the value of an annuity will grow much quicker without taxes being assessed every year. Second, since you can defer the taxes until you take a withdrawal or payments, you have the opportunity to "time the tax" by receiving money from the policy in years when other income is lower (such as retirement) or when you have significant offsetting deductions.

Deferral is not a free lunch, however, and these two advantages are somewhat offset by two disadvantages. The first is that growth within the contract (when payments or withdrawals are finally made) is taxed at ordinary income rates which can be 35% in the highest bracket, instead of the less painful 15% capital gains rates.[34] The second disadvantage is that withdrawals prior to age 59½ are subject to a 10% penalty.[35] Both of these consequences merit further discussion.

Gains Taxed as Ordinary Income

The gains from annuities are taxed at ordinary income tax rates when withdrawn. Compare this to the long-term capital gains rates for those who buy and hold securities for long periods, such as an S&P 500 fund. But this comparison really does not fit, since long-term capital investments take a different place within an investment allocation. Plus, capital investments such as an S&P 500 fund have

---

34. Note also that that most states also have income taxes, capital gains taxes, or both. A few states have neither.
35. Your original principal is never subject to taxes or penalties; only the investment growth within the EIA is subject to taxes or penalties.

the serious and very real possibility for significant losses of principal in a stock market crash or extended bear market.

Taking on significant investment risk just to get better tax treatment is certainly allowing the tax tail to wag the economics dog.[36]

For tax purposes, EIAs should instead be compared to what they are most like in terms of safety, such as government bonds and highly-rated corporate bonds. If held to maturity, the returns from these investments are also taxed at ordinary income tax rates. We say "if held to maturity" since an increase in interest rates could work to seriously devaluate even the most highly rated government and corporate bonds, meaning that you might be forced to hold these instruments to maturity to receive the yield you anticipated. So, in truth, EIAs are taxed no worse than other vehicles within their comparable asset class.

To approach the safety of EIAs, stock portfolios must be asset allocated and repeatedly re-balanced, which can create long-and short-term capital gains that are immediately taxable.[37] Stock portfolios are taxed every year that trades are made, whereas taxes paid on EIAs are typically deferred until withdrawn.[38] Depending on how actively the stock portfolio is rebalanced (which is a primarily a function of stock market volatility), the cumulative tax treatment could be devastating to performance. Moreover, if you put your money in very high-turnover investments such as with many hedge funds, you may find that the total taxes paid will be significantly worse than the taxes paid with an EIA.

---

36. What the NASD says (see Appendix A)

    Do EIAs and other tax-deferred annuities provide the same advantages as 401(k)s and other before tax retirement plans? No, 401(k) plans and other before-tax retirement savings plans not only allow you to defer taxes on income and investment gains, but your contributions reduce your current taxable income. That's why most investors should consider an EIA and other annuity products only after they make the maximum contribution to their 401(k) and other before-tax retirement plans.

37. This is in addition, of course, to trading fees and expenses.

38. What the NAIC says (see Appendix B)

    Federal income tax on interest accumulated in an annuity is deferred until you take the interest out of the annuity. You may be required to pay taxes then on the tax-deferred accumulation. You may have to pay a tax penalty if you withdraw the accumulation before you are age 59½. The advantage of tax deferral is that you will probably be in a lower tax bracket in retirement than while you are employed. Also, during the accumulation period, you will be earning interest on money that you would otherwise have used to pay taxes. Tax-qualified annuities are subject to different rules. In any case, you should consult your own tax advisor.

Penalty for Withdrawals Prior to Age 59½

Payments or loans taken from EIAs prior to age 59½ are subject to the 10% tax penalty for early withdrawals.[39] This significantly limits the types of persons for whom EIAs are suitable. We have mentioned before that an EIA should never be sold to somebody who reasonably anticipates needing the money before the end of the surrender period. An EIA is not suitable for anybody who reasonably anticipates needing the money before they turn age 59½ either. In fact, it is difficult to see how the sale of an EIA to somebody under 40 years old could ever make financial sense unless they knew they did not need the money, since they could not make a withdrawal without the penalty for at least 20 years.[40]

Partial Withdrawals and LIFO

Annuities are subject to "Last In, First Out" (LIFO) accounting. This means that if you make a partial withdrawal of your money in an EIA, the (taxable) growth within the contract will come out first, and only then will your (nontaxable) initial principal be returned to you.

Annuities Are Not Always Tax Deferred

An annuity can only be tax deferred if it is held for a natural person or in trust for the benefit of a natural person. By contrast, an annuity that is held in a corporation, limited partnership, LLC, or other business entity might not be entitled to tax deferred status. Note that this latter category may include so-called "Family Limited Partnerships"—placing annuities into such an entity requires careful prior analysis from a tax perspective.[41]

---

39. <u>What the NASD says</u> (see Appendix A)
    Also, any withdrawals from tax-deferred annuities before you reach the age of 59½ are generally subject to a 10% tax penalty in addition to any gain being taxed as ordinary income.
40. There are a limited number of special-event exceptions under §72 where a distribution prior to age 59½ will not result in a 10% penalty, such as where the owner of the annuity dies or becomes disabled before reaching age 59½.
41. See Letter Ruling 199944020 which held that a limited partnership that held an annuity for the benefit of the limited partners was "not a mere agent" for the partners, and so therefore there would be no tax deferral under tax code § 72(u) that concerns the treatment of annuity contracts not held by natural persons.

After Your Premiums Are Returned

As we mentioned earlier, at the end of the accumulation period you can elect to annuitize and start the guaranteed payments coming to you. So, how are these taxed?

Remember that the payments are calculated based on your life expectancy and spread over that period. This means that your original premium payments (called "basis" in the tax context) are calculated to last until the date of life expectancy. Until this date, when you receive payments from your annuity, you will receive a payment that is in one part a tax-free return of your original basis and one part growth that is taxed to you as ordinary income.

However, once the date of your life expectancy is reached, your basis has been exhausted and your entire payment may henceforth be treated as ordinary income. In other words, as of that date the entirety of the payments that you receive from the annuity may be treated as ordinary income and you will no longer get tax-free credit for your original purchase price that you paid.

Exchanges and Gifts

With some limitations, you can exchange your existing annuity for an EIA or other type of annuity without any immediate tax consequences. You can also exchange your life insurance policy for an EIA or other type of annuity without any immediate tax consequences (but not *vice versa*—the exchange of an annuity for a life insurance policy may trigger taxes).[42] In fact, at the end of the accumulation period, most people simply exchange their old annuity for a new annuity.

You have to be very careful when you make gifts of an annuity, since the person who receives the gift may have to pay taxes on the gain, as well as any gift taxes due. There are likely to also be issues on the contributions of annuities to trusts. Thus, you should never make the gift of an annuity to either a person or a trust without the assistance of a qualified tax professional.

Similarly, if you make the gift of an annuity to a charity, that may also trigger taxes due on the gains. You should be able to offset these taxes, however, by the charitable deduction that you will receive. Caution that the amount of the charitable deduction may be limited by your original cost basis, *i.e.*, the amount of your original premium payments into the annuity, and not the cash value. For

---

42. Such a tax-free exchange is known as a *1035 Exchange*, since it is authorized under § 1035 of the tax code. Note that there are circumstances where such an exchange may be taxable in some part, such as where the exchange is partial or where the insurance policy is subject to a loan.

this reason, it may make sense to first cash out the annuity and then contribute the proceeds to the charity.

Estate Tax Considerations

How EIAs are treated for estate tax purposes is a very complex subject that largely depends on how the payout will be made under the contract and how the EIA is positioned within your overall estate plan. You should not presume any particular treatment based on general understandings of how annuities are taxed, but instead seek the counsel of a qualified tax planner for guidance in your particular circumstances.

As with all annuities, consumers should be cautious of the combined income and estate tax issues relating to "Income in Respect to a Decedent" (IRD), where the annuitant dies before the annuity pays out. In this situation, the growth within the annuity is subject to both income taxes and estate taxes. Although there is a deduction so that these taxes are not truly cumulative, they can still be a serious gut-punch to the value of the estate. Therefore, it is critically essential that EIAs be placed within a carefully thought out estate planning structure to avoid this significant downside.

The purpose of EIAs is to fund retirement needs and spending, and not to grow the estate. If growing the estate is the primary goal, then life insurance purchased inside an Irrevocable Life Insurance Trust (known as an "ILIT") or similar estate planning trust may be a more efficient arrangement.

10
ASSET PROTECTION

Asset protection is pre-lawsuit planning that has as its goal to protect wealth from creditors should claims later arise. It is a common concern of those who are in high-risk occupations, such as physicians, and many business owners who are regularly exposed to lawsuits. Asset protection is completely proper so long as it is done in accordance with the law, and completed sufficiently in advance of claims so that the fraudulent transfer laws will not apply.

As a form of annuity contracts, the statutes of a few states protect the entire value of EIAs from creditors, while some other states protect a part of the annuity payment. For instance, Section 1108.051(b) of the Texas Insurance Code provides that:

> "[A]nnuity benefits...are fully exempt[43] from:
>
> A. garnishment, attachment, execution, or other seizure;
>
> B. seizure, appropriation, or application by any legal or equitable process or by operation of law to pay a debt or other liability of an insured or of a beneficiary, either before or after the benefits are provided; and
>
> C. a demand in a bankruptcy proceeding of the insured or beneficiary."

This basically means that if you live in Texas or another state that completely exempts annuities from collection, whatever money you have placed into an EIA (or any other form of annuity) should be protected from creditors in most cases, including in bankruptcy. Surprisingly, in the 2005 bankruptcy reform legisla-

---

43. Texas Insurance Code § 1108.053 provides three exceptions to the annuity exemption: (1) where the initial purchase of the annuity was a fraudulent transfer; (2) where the annuity itself has been pledged as security for a loan; and (3) where the debt sought to be collected is for child support.

tion[44] (which severely cut down on most other types of creditor exemptions), the exemptions for life insurance and annuities were left mostly unaffected.

Thus, annuities can be a powerful asset protection tool in some states. But what if you do not live in such a state? You then have at least two choices:

First, if a creditor appears then you could move to a state that protects annuities, so long as you do so in advance of the creditor attempting to collect on your annuity. While this is not the preferred option for protecting annuities since you might have reasons for not wanting to leave the state (such as that you might then lose your homestead protection), at least this is an option that is available to you.

Second, you could have the annuity held in one of several types of trusts that would provide asset protection benefits to the annuity. These trusts are relatively complex and expensive to form, and require the services of an experienced tax lawyer, but they do make sense to hold an EIA and other assets having significant value.

Annuities are greatly preferred for asset protection purposes over money market accounts, CDs, stocks, bonds, mutual funds, and Exchange Traded Funds (ETFs)—all of which can easily be attached by creditors in collection of a debt. In the event of an unforeseen creditor attack, these assets will be readily available to creditors and difficult to move into a protected structure because of the fraudulent transfer laws. For persons who have asset protection needs, annuities thus provide a significant non-economic benefit not offered by most other assets.

Owning Annuity in Trust

Although owning EIAs in a trust presents some tax complexities that require the use of a skilled tax lawyer, it is essential to do so where the EIA has a large value. There are several reasons for this.

The first reason is to protect the EIA from any unforeseen creditors that you might have. Even in those states where the EIA is protected by statute, placing the EIA into a trust provides an extra layer of protection in case either your state or the federal bankruptcy law later changes, or a creditor attempts an unusual maneuver such as trying to execute upon your EIA in the state where the annuity company does business to try to circumvent your state's statutory protections.

---

44. Euphemistically referred to as the "Bankruptcy Abuse Prevention and Consumer Protection Act of 2005" though there was little in the legislation that could arguably be said to protect consumers, and to the contrary nearly every provision unfavorably limited consumers' rights in one aspect or another.

The second reason is that you probably do not want your children to take the death benefit from the EIA directly, as then it would be exposed to their creditors. For instance, assume that right before your death one of your children gets into a bad car accident and is sued. The death benefit that your EIA would pay would not be protected as to your child's creditors from the car accident if paid outright. However, if the death benefit were paid into a spendthrift trust for your child's benefit, it would be protected from your child's creditors.

The third reason is—if you are wealthy—the avoidance of probate and estate taxes. While avoiding estate taxes requires complex trust structuring, the cost of doing this is usually insignificant compared to the amount of estate taxes that will be saved. Note that your EIA should not, however, be placed into a family limited partnership or LLC because then you risk losing the EIA's tax-deferred treatment.

Of course, if you live in the majority of states that do not protect EIAs, you will want to protect your EIA by placing it into a trust that has asset protective features anyway.[45]

---

45. Note that the author is not suggesting that the EIA be placed into a so-called *Asset Protection Trust* (APT), which is a self-settled spendthrift trust that you place your assets into as the settlor and then later as the beneficiary attempt to assert the spendthrift provisions to protect the trust assets from creditors. The track record of Foreign Asset Protection Trust has been dismal, with trust settlors routinely sent to jail until the trust assets were made available to creditors. While a few states (Alaska, Delaware, Missouri, Nevada, Oklahoma, Rhode Island, and Utah) have adopted legislation that allows for a Domestic Asset Protection Trust, such legislation is untested and some asset protection commentators (including your author) have expressed concern as to whether they will stand up to a determined creditor attack. In addition, the 2005 changes to the bankruptcy laws now allow for a 10-year clawback of assets transferred to a self-settled trust with the intention of defeating creditors. For all these reasons, your author suggests that Asset Protection Trusts, both foreign and domestic, should be avoided.

11

QUESTIONS AND MORE INFORMATION

Equity-Indexed Annuities are excellent products in the abstract and work for many consumers. For some consumers, however, equity-indexed annuities may not turn out to be a good purchase. These disappointed consumers will be those who discover too late that they needed their money during the surrender period or before they turned 59½, but they could not access it without penalty. These consumers should never have purchased an EIA in the first place, and a purpose of this book is to set out those circumstances in which a person should instead place their money into something that is more liquid so that they can meet their cash needs.

When you should absolutely not buy an Equity-Indexed Annuity

You should absolutely NOT buy an Equity-Indexed Annuity if:

- You anticipate needing most of your money from the Equity-Indexed Annuity during the surrender period.[46]

- You anticipate needing any amount of money from the Equity-Indexed Annuity prior to the time that you turn 59½.

- You are having difficulty understanding the fundamental terms of the Equity-Indexed Annuity being offered to you.

If any of these three conditions apply, then you should absolutely not buy an Equity-Indexed Annuity. Do not allow yourself to be placed into a contract for which your situation is unsuitable.

---

46. Again, many EIA contracts allow for limited "free withdrawals" even during the surrender period.

Particular Things That You Absolutely Must Know

You must understand at least the following contractual terms of the Equity-Indexed Annuity that you are considering buying:

- What is the financial rating of the annuity company?

- What is the minimum guaranteed interest rate return? What is the participation rate for interest crediting?

- How many years will surrender charges be charged? What are the surrender charges in each year?

- How is the annuity linked to the index? What is the participation rate for index crediting? Are there caps?

- What happens to the annuity if you die? Will the surrender charges be waived? Will your beneficiaries receive any money?

- What are the exchange options? Will you be forced to annuitize?

- Are there any tax consequences that you should know about?

- What are the moving parts to this annuity? What terms or rates does the annuity company have the right to change?

Regulation of EIAs

EIAs are typically regulated by the state insurance departments, but are not subject to SEC regulation. The real concern with EIAs not being registered is that the restrictions on how and to whom they are marketed are not as tight as if they were registered.[47] The sale of an investment security typically requires that a *suitability analysis* be made, but the rules are more lax for pure insurance products such as EIAs.[48]

---

47. What the NASD says (see Appendix A)
    Caution! Unlike variable annuities, EIAs are typically structured so that they are not securities registered with the SEC. Nor are the sales of EIAs regulated by the SEC and NASD. This means that non-registered EIAs are not subject to the customer suitability, disclosure, and sales practice requirements that registered securities are.

Recommended Reading

While this book is meant to give the common consumer a general overview of the issues involving Equity-Indexed Annuities, agents and financial planners desiring more specific product information will find Jack Marrion's "Index Annuities: Power & Protection" (Advantage Compendium 2004) to be a much more industry-oriented resource, especially as to his detailed and excellent discussion of the variances in index crediting methodology.

Similarly, those who desire to know more about annuities generally and particularly the tax treatment of annuities would be well advised to read "The Annuity Advisor" by John Olsen and Michael Kitces (National Underwriter Co., 2005), available from *Amazon.com*

Further Resources

A supporting website for this book is at *eiabook.com* which contains additional information about EIAs and other resources, such as the relevant text of Section 72 of the Internal Revenue Code which relates to annuities and cases that have discussed whether an EIA is a security. This website also has errata and *addenda* for this book, and a form for making comments or asking questions.

For questions and comments, you may also contact me directly by e-mail to *jay@eiabook.com*

For speaking engagements or paid consulting regarding EIA planning or ancillary planning, you may set up a telephone conference by calling me at 949-607-0952. You may also call me if you would like me to recommend a reputable agent to assist you with evaluating and purchasing an EIA. Please do not call me with simple comments and questions, but for that instead use the online form at eiabook.com or e-mail me.

---

48. The state insurance commissioners could and should alleviate these concerns by requiring a minimal suitability analysis, which would primarily be whether the consumer reasonably will require withdrawals prior to the end of the surrender period or before reaching age 59½. The state insurance commissioners should also require greater disclosure that withdrawals made during the surrender period could trigger penalties, and that withdrawals made before reaching age 59½ could trigger the 10% early distribution penalty. Finally, the state insurance commissioners should require a standardized format for EIA contracts and marketing brochures so that consumers could more easily compare products and their terms.

You can also write to me at:
Jay D. Adkisson
P.O. Box 7088
Laguna Niguel, CA 92677

For a much more detailed discussion of asset protection, I invite you to visit my website at *assetprotectionbook.com* and to purchase my (and Chris Riser's) "Asset Protection: Concepts and Strategies" which is available from *Amazon.com*

Regulatory Publications

I have included as appendices the informational publications about Equity-Indexed Annuities from the three regulatory agencies that dominate this area, to wit:

Appendix A	*National Association of Securities Dealers (NASD)*: "Equity-Indexed Annuities—A Complex Choice"
Appendix B	*National Association of Insurance Commissioners (NAIC)*: "Buyer's Guide to Equity-Indexed Annuities"
Appendix C	*U.S. Securities & Exchange Commission (SEC)*: "Equity-Indexed Annuities"

I strongly suggest that you read these warnings thoroughly before purchasing an Equity-Indexed Annuity. Throughout this book I have incorporated by footnotes the warnings from the NASD and NAIC in relation to specific subject-matter. I did not, however, attempt to incorporate the SEC's warnings because they were largely duplicative of those of the NASD.

APPENDIX A

National Association of Securities Dealers (NASD) Equity-Indexed Annuities—A Complex Choice

✦

June 30, 2005

Why an Alert on Equity-Indexed Annuities?

Sales of **equity-indexed annuities (EIAs)** have grown considerably in recent years. Although one insurance company includes the word "simple" in the name of their product, EIAs are anything but easy to understand. One of the most confusing features of an EIA is the method used to calculate the gain in the index to which the annuity is linked. To make matters worse, there is not one, but several different indexing methods. Because of the variety and complexity of the methods used to credit interest, investors will find it difficult to compare one EIA to another.

Before you buy an EIA, you should understand the various features of this investment and be prepared to ask your insurance agent, broker, financial planner, or other financial professional lots of questions about whether an EIA is right for you.

What is an Annuity?

An annuity is a contract between you and an insurance company in which the company promises to make periodic payments to you, starting immediately or at some future time. If the payments are delayed to the future, you have a **deferred annuity**. If the payments start immediately, you have an **immediate**

annuity. You buy the annuity either with a single payment or a series of payments called premiums.

Annuities come in two types: fixed and variable. With a **fixed annuity**, the insurance company guarantees both the rate of return and the payout. As its name implies, a **variable annuity**'s rate of return is not stable, but varies with the stock, bond, and money market funds that you choose as investment options. There is no guarantee that you will earn any return on your investment and there is a risk that you will lose money. Unlike fixed contracts, variable annuities are securities registered with the Securities and Exchange Commission (SEC). To learn more about variable annuities, read our Investor Alert, *Should You Exchange Your Variable Annuity?*

What is an Equity-Indexed Annuity?

EIAs have characteristics of both fixed and variable annuities. Their return varies more than a fixed annuity, but not as much as a variable annuity. So EIAs give you more risk (but more potential return) than a fixed annuity but less risk (and less potential return) than a variable annuity.
EIAs offer a minimum guaranteed interest rate combined with an interest rate linked to a market index. Because of the guaranteed interest rate, EIAs have less market risk than variable annuities. EIAs also have the potential to earn returns better than traditional fixed annuities when the stock market is rising.

What is the Guaranteed Minimum Return?

The guaranteed minimum return for an EIA is typically 90% of the premium paid at a 3% annual interest rate. However, if you surrender your EIA early, you may have to pay a significant surrender charge and a 10% tax penalty that will reduce or eliminate any return.

How good is this guarantee?

Your guaranteed return is only as good as the insurance company that gives it. While it is not a common occurrence that a life insurance company is unable to meet its obligations, it happens. There are several private companies that rate an insurance company's financial strength. Information about these firms can be found on the New Jersey Department of Banking & Insurance's Web site.

What is a market index?

A market index tracks the performance of a specific group of stocks representing a particular segment of the market, or in some cases an entire market. For example, the S&P 500 Composite Stock Price Index is an index of 500 stocks intended to be representative of a broad segment of the market. There are indexes for almost every conceivable sector of the stock market. Most EIAs are based on the S&P 500, but other indexes also are used. Some EIAs even allow investors to select one or more indexes.

How is an EIA's index-linked interest rate computed?

The index-linked gain depends on the particular combination of indexing features that an EIA uses. The most common indexing features are listed below. To fully understand an EIA, make sure you not only understand each feature, but also how the features work together since these features can dramatically impact the return on your investment.

- **Participation Rates.** A participation rate determines how much of the gain in the index will be credited to the annuity. For example, the insurance company may set the participation rate at 80%, which means the annuity would only be credited with 80% of the gain experienced by the index.

- **Spread/Margin/Asset Fee.** Some EIAs use a spread, margin or asset fee in addition to, or instead of, a participation rate. This percentage will be subtracted from any gain in the index linked to the annuity. For example, if the index gained 10% and the spread/margin/asset fee is 3.5%, then the gain in the annuity would be only 6.5%.

- **Interest Rate Caps.** Some EIAs may put a cap or upper limit on your return. This cap rate is generally stated as a percentage. This is the maximum rate of interest the annuity will earn. For example, if the index linked to the annuity gained 10% and the cap rate was 8%, then the gain in the annuity would be 8%.

Caution! Some EIAs allow the insurance company to change participation rates, cap rates, or spread/asset/margin fees either annually or at the start of the next contract term. If an insurance company subsequently lowers the participation rate or cap rate or increases the spread/asset/margin fees, this could adversely affect your return. Read your contract carefully to see if it allows the insurance company to change these features.

Indexing Methods. As described in the table below, there are several methods for determining the change in the relevant index over the period of the annuity. These varying methods impact the calculation of the amount of interest to be credited to the contract based on a change in the index.

Indexing Method—Description

Annual Reset (Rachet)—Compares the change in the index from the beginning to the end of each year. Any declines are ignored.

Advantage: Your gain is "locked in" each year.

Disadvantage: Can be combined with other features, such as lower cap rates and participation rates that will limit the amount of interest you might gain each year.

High Water Mark—Looks at the index value at various points during the contract, usually annual anniversaries. It then takes the highest of these values and compares it to the index level at the start of the term.

Advantage: May credit you with more interest than other indexing methods and protect against declines in the index.

Disadvantage: Because interest is not credited until the end of the term, you may not receive any index-link gain if you surrender your EIA early. It can also be combined with other features; such as lower cap rates and participation rates that will limit the amount of interest you might gain each year.

Point-to-Point—Compares the change in the index at two discrete points in time, such as the beginning and ending dates of the contract term.

Advantage: May be combined with other features, such as higher cap and participation rates, that may credit you with more interest.

Disadvantage: Relies on single point in time to calculate interest. Therefore, even if the index that your annuity is linked to is going up throughout the term of your investment, if it declines dramatically on the last day of the term, then part or all of the earlier gain can be lost. Because interest is not credited until the end of the term, you may not receive any index-link gain if you surrender your EIA early.

- **Index Averaging.** Some EIAs average an index's value either daily or monthly rather than use the actual value of the index on a specified date. Averaging may reduce the amount of index-linked interest you earn.

- **Interest Calculation.** The way that an insurance company calculates interest earned during the term of an EIA can make a big difference in the amount of money you will earn. Some EIAs pay simple interest during the term of the annuity. Because there is no compounding of interest, your return will be lower.

- **Exclusion of Dividends.** Most EIAs only count equity index gains from market price changes, excluding any gains from dividends. Since you're not earning dividends, you won't earn as much as if you invested directly in the market.

Can I get my money when I need it?

EIAs are long-term investments. Getting out early may mean taking a loss. Many EIAs have surrender charges. The surrender charge can be a percentage of the amount withdrawn or a reduction in the interest rate credited to the EIA.

Also, any withdrawals from tax-deferred annuities before you reach the age of 59½ are generally subject to a 10% tax penalty in addition to any gain being taxed as ordinary income.

Do EIAs and other tax-deferred annuities provide the same advantages as 401(k)s and other before tax retirement plans?

No, 401(k) plans and other before-tax retirement savings plans not only allow you to defer taxes on income and investment gains, but your contributions reduce your current taxable income. That's why most investors should consider an EIA and other annuity products only after they make the maximum contribution to their 401(k) and other before-tax retirement plans. To learn more about 401(k)s, please read Smart 401(k) Investing.

Is it possible to lose money in an EIA?

Yes. Many insurance companies only guarantee that you'll receive 90% of the premiums you paid, plus at least 3% interest. Therefore, if you don't receive any index-linked interest, you could lose money on your investment. One way that you could not receive any index-linked interest is if the index linked to your annuity declines. The other way you may not receive any index-linked interest is if you surrender your EIA before maturity. Some insurance companies will not credit you with index-linked interest when you surrender your annuity early.

If You Have Questions

If you have questions about EIAs, you can contact your state insurance commissioner. You can check out whether the person selling an EIA is registered with the NASD check NASD BrokerCheck or call our Hotline at (800) 289-9999.

Additional Resources

NASD Investor Alert, "*Variable Annuities: Beyond the Hard Sell*"
NASD Investor Alert, "*Should You Exchange Your Variable Annuity?*"
NASD Notice to Members 05-50, *Member Responsibilities for Supervising Sales of Unregistered Equity-Indexed Annuities*
National Association of Insurance Commissioners' *Buyer's Guide to Equity-Indexed Annuities.*
Securities and Exchange Commission's Variable Annuities: *What You Should Know.*
To receive the latest Investor Alerts and other important investor information sign up for *Investor News.*

APPENDIX B

National Association of Insurance Commissioners (NAIC) Buyer's Guide To Equity-Indexed Annuities

The National Association of Insurance Commissioners is an association of state insurance regulatory officials. This association helps the various insurance departments to coordinate insurance laws for the benefit of all consumers.

This guide does not endorse any company or policy.

This Guide has been written to help you understand annuities in general and equity-indexed annuities in particular. There are different kinds of annuities. It is important for you to understand the differences among various annuities so you can choose the kind that best fits your needs. At the end of this Guide are questions you should ask your agent or the company. Make sure you are satisfied with the answers before you make a purchase.

WHAT IS AN ANNUITY?

> An annuity is a series of income payments made at regular intervals by an insurance company in return for a premium or premiums you have paid. The most frequent use of income payments from an annuity is for retirement.
>
> An annuity is neither a life insurance nor a health insurance policy. It is not a savings account or a savings certificate. You should not buy an annuity for short-term purposes.

WHAT ARE THE DIFFERENT KINDS OF ANNUITY CONTRACTS?

Individual or Group

An individual contract covers only one or two persons. A group contract covers a specific group of people, for example, the employees of an employer.

Immediate or Deferred

An immediate annuity begins to make income payments soon after you pay the premium. The income payments from a deferred annuity start later, often many years later. Deferred annuities have an "accumulation" period, which is the time between when you start paying premiums and when income payments start. The time after income payments start is called the "payout" period.

Single Premium or Installment Premium

You pay the insurance company only one premium for a single premium annuity. You pay for an installment premium annuity through a series of payments. There are two kinds of installment premium annuities. One kind is a flexible premium contract. You can pay as much as you want, whenever you want, within set limits. The other kind is a scheduled premium contract, which specifies how much your premiums will be and how often you will pay them.

Fixed or Variable

During the accumulation period of a fixed deferred annuity, premiums (less any applicable charges) earn interest at rates set by the company or in a way spelled out in the annuity contract. The company guarantees that it will pay no less than a minimum rate of interest. During the payout phase, the amount of each income payment you receive is generally set when the payments start and does not change.

During the accumulation period of a variable annuity, premiums (less any applicable charges) are put into a separate account of the insurance company. You decide how those premiums will be invested, from stock or bond mutual fund choices. The value of the separate account, and therefore, the value of your variable annuity, varies with the investment experience of the funds you choose. There is no guarantee that you will receive all of your premiums back. There is also no guarantee that you will earn any return on your annuity. During the payout period of a variable annuity, the amount of each income payment you receive may be fixed (predetermined) or variable (changing with the value of the investments in the separate account).

National Association of Insurance Commissioners (NAIC) Buyer's Guide To Equity-Indexed Annuities

WHAT ARE EQUITY-INDEXED ANNUITIES?

An equity-indexed annuity is a fixed annuity, either immediate or deferred, that earns interest or provides benefits that are linked to an external equity reference or an equity index. The value of the index might be tied to a stock or other equity index. One of the most commonly used indexes is Standard & Poor's 500 Composite Stock Price Index (the S&P 500), which is an equity index. The value of any index varies from day to day and is not predictable.

When you buy an equity-indexed annuity you own an insurance contract. You are not buying shares of any stock of index.

While immediate equity-indexed annuities may be available, this Buyer's Guide will focus on deferred equity-indexed annuities.

HOW ARE THEY DIFFERENT FROM OTHER FIXED ANNUITIES?

An equity-indexed annuity is different from other fixed annuities because of the way it credits interest to your annuity's value. Some fixed annuities only credit interest calculated at a rate set in the contract. Other fixed annuities also credit interest at rates set from time to time by the insurance company. Equity-indexed annuities credit interest using a formula based on changes in the index to which the annuity is linked. The formula decides how the additional interest, if any, is calculated and credited. How much additional interest you get and when you get it depends on the features of your particular annuity.

Your equity-indexed annuity, like other fixed annuities, also promises to pay a minimum interest rate. The rate that will be applied will not be less than this minimum guaranteed rate even if the index-linked interest rate is lower. The value of your annuity also will not drop below a guaranteed minimum. For example, many single premium annuity contracts guarantee the minimum value will never be less than 90 percent of the premium paid, plus at least 3% in annual interest (less any partial withdrawals). The guaranteed value is the minimum amount available during a term for withdrawals, as well as for some annuitizations (see "Annuity Income Payments") and death benefits. The insurance company will adjust the value of the annuity at the end of each term to reflect any index increases.

WHAT ARE SOME OF THE CONTRACT FEATURES?

Two features that have the greatest effect on the amount of additional interest that may be credited to an equity-indexed annuity are the indexing method and the participation rate. It is important to understand the features and how they work together. The following describes some other equity-indexed annuity features that affect the index-linked formula.

Since new Equity-Indexed annuity products are being developed, the contract you are interested in may contain a feature that is not discussed in this Buyer's Guide. If this is the case, ask your agent for an explanation that you understand.

Indexing Method

The indexing method means the approach used to measure the amount of change, if any, in the index. Some of the most common indexing methods, which are explained more fully later on, include annual reset (ratcheting), high-water mark and point-to-point.

Term

The index term is the period over which index-linked interest is calculated. In most product designs, interest is credited to your annuity at the end of a term. Terms are generally from one to ten years, with six or seven years being most common. Some annuities offer single terms while others offer multiple, consecutive terms. If your annuity has multiple terms, there will usually be a window at the end of each term, typically 30 days, during which you may withdraw your money without penalty. For installment premium annuities, the payment of each premium may begin a new term for that premium.

Participation Rate

The participation rate decides how much of the increase in the index will be used to calculate index-linked interest. For example, if the calculated change in the index is 9% and the participation rate is 70%, the index-linked interest rate for your annuity will be 6.3% (9% x 70% = 6.3%). A company may set a different participation rate for newly issued annuities as often as each day. Therefore, the initial participation rate in your annuity will depend on when it is issued by the company. The company usually guarantees the participation rate for a specific period (from one year to the entire term). When that period is over, the company sets a new participation rate for the next period. Some annuities guarantee that the participation rate will never be set lower than a specified minimum or higher than a specified maximum.

Cap Rate or Cap

Some annuities may put an upper limit, or cap, on the index-linked interest rate. This is the maximum rate of interest the annuity will earn. In the example given above, if the contract has a 6% cap rate, 6%, and not 6.3%, would be credited. Not all annuities have a cap rate.

Floor on Equity Index-Linked Interest

The floor is the minimum index-linked interest rate you will earn. The most common floor is 0%. A 0% floor assures that even if the index decreases in value, the index-linked interest that you earn will be zero and not negative. As in the case of a cap, not all annuities have a stated floor on index-linked interest rates. But in all cases, your fixed annuity will have a minimum guaranteed value.

Averaging

In some annuities, the average of an index's value is used rather than the actual value of the index on a specified date. The index averaging may occur at the beginning, the end, or throughout the entire term of the annuity.

Interest Compounding

Some annuities pay simple interest during an index term. That means index-linked interest is added to your original premium amount but does not compound during the term. Others pay compound interest during a term, which means that index-linked interest that has already been credited also earns interest in the future. In either case, however, the interest earned in one term is usually compounded in the next.

Margin/Spread/Administrative Fee

In some annuities, the index-linked interest rate is computed by subtracting a specific percentage from any calculated change in the index. This percentage, sometimes referred to as the "margin," "spread," or "administrative fee," might be instead of, or in addition to, a participation rate. For example, if the calculated change in the index is 10%, your annuity might specify that 2.25% will be subtracted from the rate to determine the interest rate credited. In this example, the rate would be 7.75% (10%-2.25% = 7.75%). In this example, the company subtracts the percentage only if the change in the index produces a positive interest rate.

Vesting

Some annuities credit none of the index-linked interest or only part of it, if you take out all your money before the end of the term. The percentage that is vested, or credited, generally increases as the term comes closer to its end and is always 100% at the end of the term.

HOW DO THE COMMON INDEXING METHODS DIFFER?

Annual Reset

Index-linked interest, if any, is determined each year by comparing the index value at the end of the contract year with the index value at the start of the contract year. Interest is added to your annuity each year during the term.

High-Water Mark

The index-linked interest, if any, is decided by looking at the index value at various points during the term, usually the annual anniversaries of the date you bought the annuity. The interest is based on the difference between the highest index value and the index value at the start of the term. Interest is added to your annuity at the end of the term.

Point-to-Point

The index-linked interest, if any, is based on the difference between the index value at the end of the term and the index value at the start of the term. Interest is added to your annuity at the end of the term.

WHAT ARE SOME OF THE FEATURES AND TRADE-OFFS OF DIFFERENT INDEXING METHODS?

Generally, annuities offer *preset* combinations of features. You may have to make trade-offs to get features you want in an annuity. This means the annuity you choose may also have features you don't want.

Features	Trade-Offs
Annual Reset Since the interest earned is "locked in" annually and the index value is "reset" at the end of each year, future decreases in the index will not affect the interest you have already earned. Therefore, your annuity using the annual reset method may credit more interest than annuities using other methods when the index fluctuates up and down often during the term. This design is more likely than others to give you access to index-linked interest before the term ends.	Your annuity's participation rate may change each year and generally will be lower than that of other indexing methods. Also an annual reset design may use a cap or averaging to limit the total amount of interest you might earn each year.
High-Water Mark Since interest is calculated using the highest value of the index on a contract anniversary during the term, this design may credit higher interest than some other designs if the index reaches a high point early or in the middle of the term, then drops off at the end of the term.	Interest is not credited until the end of the term. In some annuities, if you surrender your annuity before the end of the term, you may not get index-linked interest for that term. In other annuities, you may receive index-linked interest, based on the highest anniversary value to date and the annuity's vesting schedule. Also, contracts with this design may have a lower participation rate than annuities using other designs or may use a cap to limit the total amount of interest you might earn.
Point-to-Point Since interest cannot be calculated before the end of the term, use of this design may permit a higher participation rate than annuities using other designs.	Since interest is not credited until the end of the term, typically six or seven years, you may not be able to get the index-linked interest until the end of the term.

WHAT IS THE IMPACT OF SOME OTHER PRODUCT FEATURES?

Cap on Interest Earned

While a cap limits the amount of interest you might earn each year, annuities with this feature may have other product features you want, such as annual interest crediting or the ability to take partial withdrawals. Also, annuities that have a cap may have a higher participation rate.

Averaging

Averaging at the beginning of a term protects you from buying your annuity at a high point, which would reduce the amount of interest you might earn. Averaging at the end of the term protects you against severe declines in the index and losing index-linked interest as a result. On the other hand, averaging may reduce the amount of index-linked interest you earn when the index rises either near the start or at the end of the term.

Participation Rate

The participation rate may vary greatly from one annuity to another and from time to time within a particular annuity. Therefore, it is important for you to know how your annuity's participation rate works with the indexing method. A high participation rate may be offset by other features, such as simple interest, averaging, or a point-to-point indexing method. On the other hand, an insurance company may offset a lower participation rate by also offering a feature such as an annual reset indexing method.

Interest Compounding

It is important for you to know whether your annuity pays compound or simple interest during a term. While you may earn less from an annuity that pays simple interest, it may have other features you want, such as a higher participation rate.

If there is a product feature that you do not understand, ask your agent. If you still do not understand, send the company a letter telling them that you want a written response so you can study their reply. You will be doing yourself a service!

CAN I TAKE MY MONEY OUT DURING THE TERM?

In most cases, you can take all or part of the money out of a deferred annuity at any time during the term. There may be a cost if you do. Sometimes the cost is a stated dollar amount. In other cases, you give up index-linked interest on the amount withdrawn. Some annuities do not let you make a partial withdrawal until the end of a term.

WHAT WILL IT COST ME TO TAKE MY MONEY OUT EARLY?

If you withdraw all or part of the value in your annuity before the end of the term, a *withdrawal or surrender charge* may be applied. A withdrawal charge is usually a percentage of the amount being withdrawn. The percentage may be reduced or eliminated after the annuity has been in force for a certain number of years. Sometimes the charge is a reduction in the interest rate credited to the annuity.

Some annuities credit none of the index-linked interest or only part of it if you take out all your money before the end of the term. The percentage that is vested, or credited, generally increases as the term comes closer to its end and is always 100% at the end of the term.

IS THERE ALWAYS A CHARGE TO TAKE MY MONEY OUT EARLY?

Your annuity may have a limited "free withdrawal" provision. This lets you make one or more withdrawals without charge each year. The size of the free withdrawal is limited to a set percentage of your annuity's guaranteed or accumulated value. If you make a larger withdrawal, you may pay withdrawal charges. You may also lose index-linked interest on amounts you withdraw.

Most annuities waive withdrawal charges on withdrawals made within a set number of days at the end of each term. Some annuities waive withdrawal charges if you are confined to a nursing home or diagnosed with a terminal illness. You may, however, lose index-linked interest on withdrawals.

ARE DIVIDENDS INCLUDED IN THE INDEX?

Depending on the index used, stock dividends may or may not be included in the index's value. For example, the S&P 500 is a stock price index and only considers the prices of stocks. It does not recognize any dividends paid on those stocks.

WHAT ARE SOME OTHER EQUITY-INDEXED ANNUITY CONTRACT BENEFITS?

Annuity Income Payments

One of the most important benefits of deferred annuities is the right to use the value built up during the accumulation period to provide income payments during the payout period. While income payments are usually made monthly, you can often choose more or less frequent payments. The size of income payments is based on both the accumulated value in your annuity and the annuity's "benefit rate" that is in effect when income payments begin.

The insurance company uses the benefits rate to compute the amount of income payment it will pay you for each $1,000 of accumulated value in your annuity. The benefit rate usually depends on your age and sex, and the form of annuity payment you have chosen. You can usually choose from many forms of annuity payments. You might choose payments that continue as long as you live, or as long as either you or your spouse live, or payments that continue for a set number of years.

Death Benefit

Annuities provide a variety of death benefits. The most common death benefit is either the guaranteed minimum value or the value determined by the index-linked formula.

Tax Deferral

Federal income tax on interest accumulated in an annuity is deferred until you take the interest out of the annuity. You may be required to pay taxes then on the tax-deferred accumulation. You may have to pay a tax penalty if you withdraw the accumulation before you are age 59½. The advantage of tax deferral is that you will probably be in a lower tax bracket in retirement than while you are employed. Also, during the accumulation period, you will be earning interest on money that you would otherwise have used to pay taxes. Tax-qualified annuities are subject to different rules. In any case, you should consult your own tax advisor.

HOW DO I KNOW IF AN EQUITY-INDEXED ANNUITY IS RIGHT FOR ME?

The questions listed below may help you decide which type of annuity, if any, meets your retirement planning and financial needs. You should consider what your goals are for the money you may put into the annuity. You need to think about how much risk you're willing to take with the money. Ask yourself:

- How long can I leave my money in the annuity?

- What do I expect to use the money for in the future?

- Am I interested in a variable annuity with the potential for higher earnings that are not guaranteed and willing to risk losing the principal?

- Is a guaranteed interest rate more important to me, with little or no risk of losing the principal?

- Or, am I somewhere in between these two extremes and willing to take some risks?

HOW DO I KNOW WHICH EQUITY-INDEXED ANNUITY IS BEST FOR ME?

As with any other insurance product, you must carefully consider your own personal situation and how you feel about the choices available. No single annuity design may have all the features you want. It is important to understand the features and trade-offs available so you can choose the annuity that is right for you. Keep in mind that it may be misleading to compare one annuity to another unless you compare all the other features of each annuity. You must decide for yourself what combination of features makes the most sense for you. Also, remember that it is not possible to predict the future market behavior of an index.

QUESTIONS YOU SHOULD ASK YOUR AGENT OR THE COMPANY

- What is the guaranteed minimum interest rate?

- What charges, if any, are deducted from my premium?

- What charges, if any, are deducted from my contract value?

- How long is the term?

- What is the participation rate?

- For how long is the participation rate guaranteed?

- Is there a minimum participation rate?

- Does my contract have a cap?

- Is averaging used? How does it work?

- Is interest compounded during a term?

- Is there a margin, spread, or administrative fee? Is that in addition to or instead of a participation rate?

- Which indexing method is used in my contract?

- What are the surrender charges or penalties if I want to end my contract early and take out all of my money?

- Can I get a partial withdrawal without paying charges or losing interest? Does my contract have vesting?

- Does my annuity waive withdrawal charges if I am confined to a nursing home or diagnosed with a terminal illness?

- What annuity income payment options do I have?

- What is the death benefit?

FINAL POINTS TO CONSIDER

It is very important that you choose an annuity that you understand well. The purpose of this Buyer's Guide is to help you to understand your annuity. Your agent or insurance company can guide you. Remember that the quality of service you can expect from the company and the agent should also be important to you when you buy an annuity.

When you receive your contract, read it carefully. It may offer a "free look" period for you to decide if you want to keep the contract. Ask your agent or insurance company for an explanation of anything you don't understand. If you have a specific complaint or can't get the answers you need from your agent or company, contact your state insurance department.

Appendix C

U.S. Securities & Exchange Commission (SEC) Equity-Indexed Annuities

Are you considering buying an equity-indexed annuity? This brochure explains equity-indexed annuities and provides resources for obtaining additional information.

What is an equity-indexed annuity?

An equity-indexed annuity is a special type of contract between you and an insurance company. During the accumulation period—when you make either a lump sum payment or a series of payments—the insurance company credits you with a return that is based on changes in an equity index, such as the S&P 500 Composite Stock Price Index. The insurance company typically guarantees a minimum return. Guaranteed minimum return rates vary. After the accumulation period, the insurance company will make periodic payments to you under the terms of your contract, unless you choose to receive your contract value in a lump sum.

Can you lose money buying an equity-indexed annuity?

You can lose money buying an equity-indexed annuity, especially if you need to cancel your annuity early. Even with a guarantee, you can still lose money if your guarantee is based on an amount that's less than the full amount of your purchase payments. In many cases, it will take several years for an equity-index annuity's minimum guarantee to "break even."

You also may have to pay a significant surrender charge and tax penalties if you cancel early. In addition, in some cases, insurance companies may not credit you with index-linked interest if you do not hold your contract to maturity.

What are some of the contract features of equity-indexed annuities?

Equity-indexed annuities are complicated products that may contain several features that can affect your return. You should fully understand how an equity-indexed annuity computes its index-linked interest rate before you buy. An insurance company may credit you with a lower return than the actual index's gain. Some common features used to compute an equity-indexed annuity's interest rate include:

- *Participation Rates.* The participation rate determines how much of the index's increase will be used to compute the index-linked interest rate. For example, if the participation rate is 80% and the index increases 9%, the return credited to your annuity would be 7.2% (9% x 80% = 7.2%).

- *Interest Rate Caps.* Some equity-indexed annuities set a maximum rate of interest that the equity-indexed annuity can earn. If a contract has an upper limit, or cap, of 7% and the index linked to the annuity gained 7.2%, only 7% would be credited to the annuity.

- *Margin/Spread/Administrative Fee.* The index-linked interest for some annuities is determined by subtracting a percentage from any gain in the index. This fee is sometimes called the "margin," "spread," or "administrative fee." In the case of an annuity with a "spread" of 3%, if the index gained 9%, the return credited to the annuity would be 6% (9%-3% = 6%).

Another feature that can have a dramatic impact on an equity-indexed annuity's return is its indexing method (or how the amount of change in the relevant index is determined). Some common indexing methods include:

- *Annual Reset (or Ratchet).* This method credits index-linked interest based on any increase in index value from the beginning to the end of the year.

- *Point-to-Point.* This method credits index-linked interest based on any increase in index value from the beginning to the end of the contract's term.

- *High Water Mark.* This method credits index-linked interest based on any increase in index value from the index level at the beginning of the contract's term to the highest index value at various points during the contract's term, often annual anniversaries of when you purchased the annuity.

These and other features may be included in an equity-indexed annuity you are considering. Before you decide to buy an equity-indexed annuity, you should understand how each feature works and what impact, together with other features, it may have on the annuity's potential return.

Are equity-indexed annuities registered with the Securities and Exchange Commission?

Equity-indexed annuities combine features of traditional insurance products (guaranteed minimum return) and traditional securities (return linked to equity markets). Depending on the mix of features, an equity-indexed annuity may or may not be a security. The typical equity-indexed annuity is not registered with the SEC.

Who should I contact if I have a problem?

If you have a problem with an equity-indexed annuity, you should contact your state insurance commissioner. In addition, we would also like to hear from you, although we will likely only have jurisdiction to resolve your particular issue if your equity-indexed annuity is a security. You can send us your complaint using our online complaint form at *www.sec.gov/complaint.shtml*
    You can also reach us by regular mail at:
        Securities and Exchange Commission
        Office of Investor Education and Assistance
        100 F Street, N.E.
        Washington, D.C. 20549-0213

Where can I find more information?

Before you purchase an equity-indexed annuity, you should understand how it works, what factors to consider in making your decision, and how you can avoid common problems. An "investor alert" concerning equity-indexed annuities is available on the NASD's website.
    For more information about investing wisely and avoiding fraud, please check out the Investor Information section of our website at *www.sec.gov/investor.shtml*
    We have provided this information as a service to investors. It is neither a legal interpretation nor a statement of SEC policy. If you have questions concerning the meaning or application of a particular law or rule, please consult with an attorney who specializes in securities law.
    This page is: *http://www.sec.gov/investor/pubs/equityidxannuity.htm*

Index

absolute return 8, 36
accumulation period 24, 42, 44, 60, 68, 71
accumulation phase 4, 41
accumulation process 24
administrative fee 15, 16, 63, 70, 72
Administrative Fees 15
annual interest cap 14
Annual Reset 19, 20, 56, 64, 65, 72
annual reset 12, 14, 19, 20, 62, 65, 66
annuitization 4
annuitize 7, 24, 26, 44, 50
annuitized 6, 25
annuity company ratings 28
annuity payments 2, 4, 24, 26, 35, 68
Annuity Stream 24
asset allocated portfolio 37
asset allocation analysis 36, 38
Asset protection 46
asset protection vii, viii, 35, 47, 48, 52
Averaging 14, 56, 63, 66
averaging 14, 20, 63, 65, 66, 70

Backtested 17
backtested 17
bankruptcy 46, 47, 48
beneficiary 25, 46, 48

capital gains 41, 42
Caps 14, 15, 72
caps 13, 14, 15, 16, 20, 21, 22, 23, 50
cash and equivalents 36, 37
CDs 37, 38, 47

Certificates of Deposit 36
commissions 6
Complexity 30, 31, 32
complexity 2, 31, 32, 53
compounded interest 9
contract anniversary 19, 20, 21, 65
crediting rates 9

Death Benefit 25, 68
death benefit 25, 48, 68, 70
declared rate fixed annuity 3
deferred annuity 4, 24, 34, 53, 60, 66
Disclosure 30, 31
distribution phase 4
diversification xi, 19, 28
Dividends 16, 57
dividends 16, 17, 57, 67

early distribution penalty 11
early withdrawal 5, 6, 24, 33
early withdrawals 36, 38, 43
estate planning 30, 45
estate tax 45

family limited partnership 48
Family Limited Partnerships 43
financial needs 30, 31, 36, 68
fixed annuity 3, 4, 5, 12, 25, 36, 54, 61, 63
fraudulent transfer 46, 47

guaranteed minimum rate 25
guaranteed payments 25, 26, 44

hedge funds 42
High Water Mark 20, 21, 56, 72

ILIT 45
Income in Respect to a Decedent 45
income tax 41, 42, 68
Index Crediting 10, 12
index crediting 8, 12, 50, 51
index funds 39, 40
index method 18
index rates 10
Index Shares 39
index shares 27, 39, 40
indexing method 12, 14, 18, 21, 61, 62, 66, 70, 72
indexing methods 12, 18, 19, 20, 21, 23, 53, 56, 62, 65, 72
index-linked rate 25
index-linked return 15
inflation 31, 37, 38
installment payments 26
Interest Crediting 8, 10
interest crediting 10, 12, 15, 50, 66
interest rates 10, 23, 38, 42, 63
internal charges 3
investment risks 36
Irrevocable Life Insurance Trust 45

Jack Marrion's 51
John Olsen 51
Joint and Survivor 26

laddered 37
Last In, First Out 43
Life Annuity, With Refund 26
Life Only, No Refund 25
LIFO 43
liquidity 33, 34, 36, 38
Lockboxing 34

loss of principal 9, 17, 33, 40
lump sum distribution 26

Mandatory Annuitization 26
margin 15, 16, 55, 63, 70, 72
Margins 15
Maturity Date 7
maximum return 12
medium-term bonds 38
Michael Kitces 51
minimum crediting rates 9
minimum guaranteed interest rate 29, 50, 54
minimum guaranteed rate 8, 9, 61
minimum interest rate 37, 61, 69
money market accounts 36, 37, 38, 47
money market funds 1, 38, 54
Moving Parts 29
moving parts 2, 29, 50
mutual fund xi, 16, 39, 60
Mutual Funds 39
mutual funds xi, 3, 35, 39, 47

NASD vii, xii, 10, 13, 14, 15, 16, 20, 21, 22, 27, 33, 42, 43, 50, 52, 53, 58, 73

ordinary income 41, 42, 43, 44, 57

Partial Withdrawals 43
participation rate 10, 12, 13, 14, 15, 16, 20, 21, 22, 50, 55, 61, 62, 63, 65, 66, 69, 70, 72
Participation rates 13
participation rates 10, 15, 16, 20, 21, 22, 23, 55, 56
Point-to-Point 22, 23, 56, 64, 65, 72
premium bonus 10

ratchet 19
reset 19, 20, 65

S 4, 16, 41
S 500 12, 16, 55, 61, 67, 71
SEC xii, 50, 52, 54, 71, 73
segregated reserves 27
simple interest 9, 10, 14, 56, 63, 66
spread 3, 15, 16, 22, 26, 44, 55, 63, 70, 72
Spreads 15
stock portfolios 42
style drift 39
suitability 1, 6, 17, 30, 32, 33, 50
Surrender Charges 5
surrender charges 1, 6, 24, 33, 50, 57, 70
Surrender Period 6

Tax deferral 41
tax deferred 39, 43
tax-deferred 24, 37, 41, 42, 43, 48, 57, 68
tax-free exchange 25, 44
Tax-Free Exchanges 25
time the tax 39, 41
Trust Me 31

unsuitable 2, 30, 38, 49

variable annuities 3, 5, 27, 50, 54
variable annuity 5, 25, 31, 54, 60, 69

1035 Exchange 25, 44

978-0-595-40418-6
0-595-40418-9

Lightning Source UK Ltd.
Milton Keynes UK
174474UK00002B/155/A